D0578742

LAYER CAKES *and* SHEET CAKES

ALSO BY LISA YOCKELSON

The Efficient Epicure

Glorious Gifts from Your Kitchen

Fruit Desserts

Brownies and Blondies

Baking for Gift-Giving

Cobblers, Crisps, and Deep-Dish Pies

A Country Baking Treasury

American Baking Classics

LAYER CAKES
and
SHEET CAKES

LISA YOCKELSON

HarperCollins*Publishers*

 For information address HarperCollins Publishers, Inc., 10 East 53rd Street, New York, NY 10022.

HarperCollins books may be purchased for educational, business, or sales promotional use. For information please write: Special Markets Department, HarperCollins Publishers, Inc., 10 East 53rd Street, New York, NY 10022.

FIRST EDITION

Designed by Helene Wald Berinsky

Library of Congress Cataloging-in-Publication Data

Yockelson, Lisa.
Layer cakes and sheet cakes / Lisa Yockelson.
p. cm. — (American baking classics)
Includes index.
ISBN 0-06-017195-2
1. Cake. 2. Baking. I. Title. II. Series.
TX771.Y645 1996
641.8'653—dc20 96-10485

96 97 98 99 00 ❖/RRD 10 9 8 7 6 5 4 3 2 1

Contents

ACKNOWLEDGMENTS

Remembering and baking (again) those remarkable layer cakes made during my childhood years surely inspired and enhanced the creation of this cookbook. Yet it's the continuing encouragement of individuals vital to the publishing process that guided these recipes into print, coddled the manuscript, and, finally, sent this book (as well as the previous volumes in my American Baking Classics series) along its way. With admiration for their skillful ways, they are: Susan Friedland, my editor and director of cookbook publishing at HarperCollins; Susan Lescher of the Lescher Agency, Inc., my literary agent; Joseph Montebello, creative director at HarperCollins; Jennifer Griffin, associate editor at HarperCollins; Wende Gozan, former publicist at HarperCollins; Sherri Steinfeld, freelance publicist; and Carolyn Larson, assistant to Susan Lescher at the Lescher Agency, Inc.

And for their individual and collective expertise in my office, kitchen, and garden, I prize the work of Eric Shangold, computer specialist and consultant, Daniel Magruder of Voell Custom Kitchens, and Roger Lowery at Bryant and Lowery Landscape Management.

LAYER CAKES
and
SHEET CAKES

1

The Appeal of Homemade Cakes

The words *homemade cake* recall the image of freshly baked layers, one stacked on top of the other and wrapped in a creamy frosting. Those layers would be soft and moist, and the frosting a rich wrapping for the delicate cake. No other sweet is exactly like an American layer cake, for the texture and grain of the cake, usually created by the definitive "creaming method," is a feathery work of art and, as desserts go, dreamy and soothing.

For a layer cake, the batter is baked in 8-, 9-, or 10-inch round baking pans; the resulting cake layers are cooled and topped with frosting. Most unbaked batters are remarkably smooth, light, and soft (with a texture that practically resembles a buttercream) and some are thinner but still silky and lustrous. A marvelous scent fills the kitchen as the layers bake and, in a short time, they are ready to receive a coating of frosting or icing. Whether the allure is one of sentiment or taste, the time-honored layer cake still pleases—the contrast of soft cake and suave frosting is simply irresistible. This is the kind of cake that entices you with its looks alone—standing tall on a cake plate or pedestal, it's the sweet promise of a home-baked dessert that's really so tempting.

Slices of layer cake look beautiful on large dessert plates, and can be presented at the conclusion of a meal or as a mid-afternoon or evening treat served with a hot or iced beverage.

The sheet cake—a must at birthdays, dinners where many cooks participate, picnics, school and charity bake sales—combines cake and frosting in a simple, single 13 by 9-inch (or 9 by 9-inch) layer. This is a transportable cake. It cuts into manageable squares, either large or small, and can be covered over with a thick frosting, a pourable glaze, or a few shakes of confectioners' sugar.

To be sure, the sheet cake is one of the workhorses of the baking kitchen, for its uncomplicated assembly and serve-directly-from-the-pan convenience is a blessing to anyone who bakes. Of the two types of cake, a sheet cake appears a dash more homespun, but tastes no less delicious.

The sweets that you'll encounter in this book, all old and new favorites of mine, are festive, not fancy cakes. Each has a genuine flavor, having been created with basic ingredients, and represents good baking, pure and simple.

2

The Cake Pantry

Cake baking, in its most elementary form, functions very well with a standard mix of ingredients, all of which are available at the market. This includes good bar chocolate, plump vanilla beans, and decent heavy cream, once considered deluxe commodities. Stock up on flours, sweeteners, extracts, leavening, and spices and keep them stored together in a cabinet for easy accessibility (consider this your baking shelf). Ground spices and baking powder should be checked from time to time to confirm freshness, for, with age, spices lose their pungency and old baking powder is ineffective in elevating batters.

In my pantry, several shelves accommodate baking supplies exclusively, stored in their own packaging or transferred into storage containers. Bar chocolate, cocoa, extracts, syrups, honey, and such remain in their foil, can, glass, or paper wrappings, but I usually transfer light or dark brown sugar, cornstarch, baking soda, baking powder (if not already purchased in a self-sealing can), and dried fruit into sturdy storage containers with tight-fitting lids to keep it all fresh and appealing. And since I bake so much, all-purpose and cake flours, granulated sugar and confectioners' sugar, and some special ingredients (such as maple sugar) are stored in glass apothecary jars on my kitchen countertop so that I can reach them easily and see when supplies are low.

Stocking the pantry with the basics and storing baking supplies within easy reach streamlines the baking process.

These are the items that I rely on to make excellent cakes:

Flour

The recipes in this book use either bleached all-purpose flour and/or bleached cake flour. Bleached flour gives the baked cake a finer, more delicate "crumb." All-purpose flour is available in 5- and 10-pound bags and cake flour in 2-pound boxes. To answer the question of so many readers about the brands of flour I use in baking: I use Gold Medal all-purpose flour and Swan's Down cake flour.

Grains

The Oatmeal Cake on page 68 is made with "quick-cooking" (not instant) rolled oats. The "quick-cooking" oats are soaked in boiling water before they are added to the batter, a technique that creates a supple, downy texture in that particular sheet cake.

Sweeteners

A variety of sugars, alone or in combination with one another, are used routinely in layer cakes and sheet cakes. They are: plain granulated sugar (packaged in 5- and 10-pound bags); superfine sugar (also know as "bar" or "dessert" sugar and available in 1-pound boxes); light brown sugar and dark brown sugar, available in 1-pound boxes (to measure, firmly press the sugar into cups used for measuring dry ingredients); and confectioners' sugar, also known as powdered sugar (available in 1-pound boxes). Granulated and superfine sugar should flow easily and brown sugar should be free of any hard lumps. If you have any doubts about the uniform texture of either light or dark brown sugar, strain it before measuring, for bits of hardened sugar will surely remain in the batter and ruin the texture of the baked cake.

For easy reference, know that a 1-pound box of confectioners' sugar contains approximately 4 cups of sugar; a 1-pound box of superfine sugar yields about 2⅓ cups; and a 1-pound box of either light or dark brown sugar holds about 2¼ packed cups.

Butter, shortening, and oil

Cakes with the most delicate grain and gossamer texture are made with fresh (*not* frozen and defrosted) unsalted butter, solid shortening (such as Crisco), or a mixture of the two. The character of butter is altered during the process of freezing and defrosting, and the change is reflected in the texture of the baked cake. On testing, cakes baked with frozen, defrosted, and softened butter yielded a denser, more compact cake, with a heavier "crumb." This quality is more obvious in layer and sheet cakes (made by the "creamed" method), and less conspicuous in bar cookies, such as brownies or blondies, when the butter is used in the melted state and the texture of the final product is dense, fudgy, or chewy. The Spiced Carrot Cake (page 64) uses plain vegetable oil (choose soybean or canola), as opposed to butter or shortening, which gives the baked cake a divinely moist texture.

Milk, cream, and cream cheese

Cakes and frostings use whole milk, evaporated milk (available in 5-ounce cans), half-and-half, buttermilk, light cream, sour cream, and cream cheese (available in 3-ounce and 8-ounce packages).

Eggs

All of the recipes in this book use extra-large eggs.

Leavenings

Baking powder and baking soda, the choice, time-honored leavening agents, should always be measured in level amounts. Dip the measuring spoon into a container and sweep off the excess with the straight edge of a smooth-surfaced, flat table knife or, preferably, a flexible palette knife. If your baking soda is lumpy, lightly press out the lumps before measuring; actually sieving the baking soda might alter the quantity and so leaven the cake improperly. It's wise to purchase baking powder in small quantities and replace it within 6 to 9 months in order to assure freshness. Store both baking powder and baking soda away from any direct heat source, in sturdy storage jars with tight-fitting lids.

Extracts

Pure extracts contribute the best flavor and aroma to baked goods. The cake recipes in this book make appropriate use of vanilla extract and occasional use of almond extract and lemon extract.

Spices

Aromatic and full of intense flavor, a ground spice both colors and brightly seasons a cake batter. Spices are usually sifted along with the flour and leavening(s). With the exception of salt, it is essential to store spices in a reasonably cool, dark place.

The scent of spices past their prime is dull, and old spices are not worthy of adding to a batter; fresh spices, however, are pungent and zesty. Cinnamon, allspice, nutmeg, cloves, ginger, and cardamom are used alone or as a medley in layer cakes and sheet cakes. Since bottled ground nutmeg has a lackluster taste, I grate whole nutmegs as needed for each recipe on a nutmeg grater. It's easy enough to do and vastly improves the taste of the finished cake. (A nutmeg grater is a small, arched section of metal, with fine holes and a built-in back or top pocket for accommodating two or three whole nutmegs.)

Nuts

Nuts, fresh or dried fruit, and vegetables add character to baked goods and, frequently, identify and distinguish a particular cake. The cakes and frostings in this book make occasional use of almonds, pecans, English walnuts, and macadamia nuts.

Most nuts, and especially walnuts and pecans, benefit by a preparatory roasting in the oven to bring out their full flavor before they are added to a cake batter. To do this, scatter the nuts on a rimmed baking sheet, such as a jelly-roll pan, and place them in a preheated 350-degree oven for about 5 to 7 minutes. The nuts should give off a gentle aroma, and turn slightly darker; walnuts will darken to a tawny brown and pecans to a slightly more burnished brown. Always keep a watchful eye on the nuts during baking, as they tend to burn quickly. Cool the nuts completely before chopping and adding to a batter or frosting.

Regarding storage, nuts hold perfectly in the refrigerator for about 2 months when packed in lidded containers, although they should be tasted before using to verify freshness. Walnuts and pecans can be frozen for longer storage, about 9 months.

Fruit and vegetables

The carrot cake is perhaps the most popular vegetable-based American cake; apple and banana cakes maximize the use of basic, staple fruit. For the cakes in this book, apples and carrots are shredded, bananas are mashed, pumpkin is used in its pureed form (easily purchased in 1-pound cans), and blueberries are simply picked over for stems and leaves, and rinsed. Other items used in cake baking: crushed pineapple in natural juices (available in 8-ounce cans), sweetened flaked coconut (available in 7-ounce bags), and dark raisins.

Chocolate and chocolate candy bars

American cake batters and frostings do incorporate ample amounts of chocolate—in the form of unsweetened chocolate, unsweetened cocoa powder, miniature and standard-size semisweet chocolate chips, semisweet and bittersweet chocolate, and candy bars sometimes fortified with nuts.

Chocolate, in all of the following forms, is easy to shop for at the supermarket: Unsweetened chocolate (available in 8-ounce boxes, each square weighing 1 ounce); semisweet chocolate (available in 8-ounce boxes, each square weighing 1 ounce); semisweet chocolate chips (available in 12-ounce bags); miniature semisweet chocolate chips (available in 12-ounce bags); semisweet mint-flavored chocolate chips (available in 10-ounce bags); bittersweet bar chocolate, such as Lindt Excellence or Tobler Tradition (available in 3-ounce bars); Baker's German's Sweet Chocolate Bar (available in 4-ounce bars); and chocolate-covered almond toffee candy (available in 1.4-ounce bars).

Many food emporiums carry Valrhona chocolate, produced in France, and Callebaut bittersweet chocolate, a product of Belgium. The Valrhona Equatoriale, a dark bittersweet chocolate (couverture), is one of my very favorite types to use when melted or chunked bittersweet chocolate is called for in a recipe. The 3-ounce bittersweet bar chocolates mentioned above can be found at major markets, and work well in any of the cake recipes, but it is worth a special trip to buy either the Callebaut or Valrhona chocolate to have on hand. Store chocolate, well wrapped, in a cool pantry.

3

Supplies for Cake Baking

To create layer cakes and sheet cakes with that distinctively delicate texture and fine, even-grained "crumb," you need to use the proper equipment, in addition to good-quality ingredients and proven techniques. As an example, proper baking pans—in size and weight—will yield downy, golden layers, with even edges all around, while incorrectly sized pans will encourage the batter to overflow or bake into an undersized shape. The following equipment, integral to a working baking kitchen, will last and last, and assure you some very fine baked goods.

MEASURING TOOLS

A set of graduated measuring spoons is the requisite device for dividing out amounts of baking powder, baking soda, salt, ground spices, and extracts. Typically, these are attached to a ring. Both beginning and seasoned bakers can use several sets of measuring spoons. *Nested graduated measuring cups* are the only choice for measuring dry ingredients (flour, sugar, cornstarch, and so on). *Liquid measuring cups*, made of glass or heavy-duty plastic, have line markings that designate the levels of measurement in cups and ounces, and are used for measuring milk, cream, buttermilk, syrups, molasses, sour cream, and such.

MIXERS

For cake baking, an electric mixer on a stand is simply the most practical and effective way to create a silky, gossamer batter from modest pantry staples. Batters that are improperly beaten rarely achieve tenderness once baked, so a reliable mixer is a sound investment for anyone who bakes. Creaming butter and sugar and beating eggs are two important tasks that a mixer accomplishes easily, and in a smooth, streamlined fashion. An electric hand mixer is a practical device for combining ingredients for cake frostings; it's usually equipped with at least three speeds. A hand mixer is essential for preparing any frosting or icing that must be beaten in a double boiler over barely simmering water.

CAKE PANS

The cakes in this book are baked in 8-inch round baking pans (1½ inches high); 9-inch round baking pans (1½ to 1¾ inches high); 10-inch round baking pans (1½ inches high); a rectangular 13 by 9 by 2-inch pan; and a 9 by 9 by 2-inch square pan. Ideally, it's best to use medium-weight aluminum pans, which form a patina over the years you bake batters in them. The corners of my rectangular and square pans have distinct, straight edges, and these pans produce cakes which can be cut into precise squares or rectangles. Round-edged square or rectangular pans function well, too, although the four corner pieces of cake have curved sides, and the entire pan slants outward.

All layer cake pans are lightly greased, the bottoms are lined with circles of wax paper, and the sides are coated with a haze of all-purpose flour. Rectangular or square baking pans are just greased and floured, as the baked and frosted cakes will remain in the pan for cutting and serving.

WAX PAPER

It's no secret—I just love wax paper. This light but sturdy culinary tool makes an ideal surface onto which you can easily measure and sift dry ingredients. (The sheets of wax paper used for measurement can be used over again;

fold them and store right in the sifter.) As cake pan liners, rounds of wax paper are thin and practically weightless, as efficient as parchment paper, and, for layer cake pans, just as practical at a fraction of the cost. For convenience, you can cut out rounds of wax paper in various round sizes and store them directly in clean layer cake pans.

Wax paper is also useful for achieving an excellent, finished bottom edge to frosted or iced layer cakes: Cut four strips of wax paper about 3 to 4 inches wide. Place the strips on a cake plate in the shape of a square (the center will be a framed square with some of the plate showing), then set on the layers and frost as usual. When the frosting has firmed up, normally in about 1 hour, gently remove the strips of wax paper by lightly pulling each away from the cake, one at a time.

FLEXIBLE RUBBER SPATULAS

Although a rubber spatula is most frequently used for pushing batter from the sides of a mixing bowl, this indispensable piece of baking equipment also makes swift and facile work of combining ingredients into mixtures, such as melted butter and chocolate, and folding egg whites through a batter. I rely on the small size (6-inch-long handle, with a blade 2 inches wide and 3½ inches long) for general combining and scraping, and the large size (9-inch-long handle, with a blade 2¾ inches wide and 4½ inches long) for blending egg whites into batters and mixing full-size batters. Buy several sizes of each to have on hand, to avoid tedious washing and drying of the spatulas at each baking session.

METAL COOLING RACKS

The purpose of a cooling rack is to permit air to cross underneath the cake pan itself and, later, around and about each inverted cake layer once it has been released from the cake pan. Good air flow circulating about the layers will guard against dampness. Cake layers must be cool and free of moisture before frosting or icing is applied to them, to preserve the texture of the cake and the creaminess of the frosting. (Damp layers become gummy and taste as if the batter was underbaked.) Sturdy cooling racks that are well constructed will last a lifetime.

Several metal cooling racks are a must for the final stage of the cake-baking process. A rectangular rack is made of criss-crossing grids, and a round rack is constructed of circular spirals of metal. Round cake racks should be purchased to accommodate 10-inch cake layers (and will, of course, hold all smaller layers) with an extra 2 to 4 inches of space for ease in handling; thus you'll need to own 12- or 14-inch cooling racks. Since sheet cakes are baked and cut in the pan, you'll need a rack that is large enough to support a 13 by 9 by 2-inch cake pan.

FLEXIBLE PALETTE KNIFE

A thin metal palette knife with a 4½-inch offset blade is helpful for spreading and smoothing frosting over the top of a sheet cake or over and between layers of cake. "Offset" indicates that the blade is set away from the handle, which allows the baker to smooth over the frosting without marring the surface.

RULER AND SCISSORS

Keep a ruler in a kitchen drawer for taking the measurement of pan sizes, and a sharp pair of scissors at hand for cutting circles of wax paper.

A DEPENDABLE TIMER

A minute timer is an important tool in any kitchen, baking or otherwise. Set the timer for about 5 to 7 minutes short of the *suggested* baking time in a particular recipe, in order to keep a careful check on the progress of the cake as it bakes. If possible, test the ring of the timer before you purchase it; the louder and longer the ring, the better.

4

Reliable Baking Techniques and Methods

Baking a beautifully textured cake, plump and beaming that undeniably sweet scent, is an art which is easy to accomplish and, at the very least, fascinating to learn and put into practice. As a result of baking so many cakes throughout the years, I've collected an inventory of quirks, watch points, and observations during my scrutiny of every phase of working with fats, sugars, leavenings, liquids, flours, and other essential ingredients.

One of the most common—and conventional—procedures for preparing a cake batter is by the "creamed" method, and that style is used regularly in the recipes that follow. The steps are simple and straightforward and, when considered, produce a cake with a most delicate grain and tantalizing flavor. Within these details lurk all those hints and tips that will assure your mastery of the cake-baking process:

ASSEMBLING THE INGREDIENTS

Measure out all liquid and dry ingredients scrupulously, using level measurements. Glass measuring cups should be used for liquids (milk, buttermilk, and so on) and soft dairy products (such as sour cream), and nested metal measuring cups for dry ingredients. The metal cups will allow you to fill them to slightly overflowing and level off the top with the straight edge of a palette knife.

Other items that must be prepared, such as chopped nuts, melted or grated chocolate (if the recipe calls for that procedure), or shredded or diced fruit and vegetables, should be readied before you actually begin to put together the cake batter.

PREPARING THE BAKING PANS

Just a few years ago, as I was putting together a batter for a layer cake, I had only enough butter to use in the recipe and not a tablespoon more. Usually, in my kitchen, cake pans are buttered and floured. Lacking the butter, I smeared a light coating of solid shortening on the inside of the pan and then proceeded to line and flour the pans. The solid shortening actually did a better job in releasing the baked cake than butter, and so my recommendation to you is to use shortening in place of butter for preparing both layer and sheet cake pans.

For layer cake pans, lightly coat the inside with a film of solid shortening. Press a circle of wax paper in the bottom of the pan, then dust a haze of all-purpose flour around the sides of the pan. (This amount is always *in addition to* the fat and flour called for in the recipe.) Invert the cake pan and tap out any excess flour over the kitchen sink.

For one-layer sheet cake pans, simply grease and flour the pan. Since the cake is cut directly from the pan, it is unnecessary to line the bottom with wax paper.

Baker's Joy, a spray that contains both vegetable oil and flour, is a fast, convenient product which virtually eliminates the act of greasing and flouring cake pans. It is usually stocked in the baking aisle of the market, along with the other release sprays, cooking oils, leavenings, and flours. Spray it evenly on the inside of layer cake and sheet cake pans. For layer cake pans, I still smooth a circle of wax paper on the bottom of each pan, for that extra bit of protection.

SIFTING THE DRY INGREDIENTS

The act of sifting the dry ingredients with the leavening (baking powder, baking soda, or a combination of both), spices (if used), and salt serves to blend the ingredients and aerate the mixture. For the success of some cakes, it is necessary to sift the ingredients more than once, to achieve a feathery texture. Sift and resift the ingredients onto sheets of wax paper; wax paper is easy to lift and pour from, and can be used over again on the next baking day. Keep the sheets, folded, directly in the sifter, and store it in a food-safe plastic bag on a cabinet shelf.

CREAMING THE BUTTER AND/OR SHORTENING

One of the most critical stages in baking is the thorough beating of the fat(s). Soften the butter at room temperature before using; the proper texture of the butter should be softly spreadable, rather than warm or oily. For "creamed" butter cake batters, the butter or solid shortening, or a mixture of both, should be beaten until supple and malleable. When correctly beaten, it should have the consistency of a medium-weight mayonnaise, and to achieve this state, count on creaming the fat on moderate speed for 3 to 5 minutes.

BEATING IN THE SUGAR

Add the sugar by degrees, that is, in small batches. When all of the sugar has been incorporated, the mixture will look somewhat white in appearance and well blended. Some bakers use the catch-all words "light and fluffy" to describe the final look of the creamed fat and sugar, a phrase which is archaic and imprecise. Does the butter and sugar mixture actually turn into something that has a fluffy texture? Not really. Beat the sugar into the fat in several portions, and after all of the sugar has been added, continue to beat the mixture for 2 to 5 minutes longer (depending upon the amount of fat and sugar called for in the recipe). This continuous mixing will give you a cake with a smooth, uniform "crumb" and beautiful, refined grain.

BEATING IN THE EGGS (OR EGG YOLKS)

Whole eggs or egg yolks are usually mixed into the batter one at a time, to allow for a thorough beating, and to build the volume of the batter. Always scrape down the sides of the mixing bowl with a rubber spatula after each egg is added to maintain a consistent texture.

ADDING THE SIFTED INGREDIENTS AND LIQUID (OR SOFT DAIRY PRODUCTS SUCH AS SOUR CREAM OR YOGURT)

Typically, in traditional baking, sifted ingredients are added to a beaten fat-sugar-egg mixture alternately with the liquid, *beginning and ending with the sifted mixture*. Incorporating the sifted mixture in this fashion is a safeguard against baking a finished cake with a coarse texture and uneven "crumb." The dry ingredients are added in two or three parts, and the liquid in one or two parts. If the liquid is added initially to the fat-sugar-egg blend, it tends to encourage the fat to break down. By adding the flour first and last, you are both preventing the batter from separating (or "curdling") and allowing the flour mixture to soak up the liquid ingredients evenly.

INCORPORATING BEATEN EGG WHITES INTO A CAKE BATTER

If egg yolks alone are mixed into a fat-and-sugar mixture, and the whites are added at the final stage, the whites must then be beaten to a firm, moist (but not dry) state. To do this, beat the whites in a clean, dry bowl, preferably stainless steel, until quite foamy, then continue beating until the peaks hold their shape. When beaten correctly, dipping a beater into the whites and bringing it up and beyond the surface of the bowl will produce a peak that stands without collapsing. (Note: If the whites are overbeaten until they are very dry, not simply firm and moist, the baked cake may be coarse-textured.)

Stir about one quarter of the egg whites into the batter to lighten it, then fold in the remaining whites, using a definite over-and-under mixing action. For this procedure, select a large spatula, a large flat whisk, or the biggest mixing spoon you can find. The whites should be fully blended into the batter without deflating it too much; little flecks of beaten egg white can remain, but be sure to break up any clumps of beaten whites the size of a whole, unshelled walnut.

FILLING THE CAKE PANS

Pour or spoon the batter into the prepared cake pans. When filling layer cake pans, you can divide up the amount of batter by eye, or, for greater precision, place each pan on a scale and fill it up in even weights. With a few quick strokes, lightly spread the batter in the pan using a thin palette knife or a rubber spatula. Resist the urge to smooth over the top of the batter more than once or twice.

BAKING THE CAKE LAYERS OR SHEET CAKE

When setting layer cake pans in the oven, stagger them on level oven shelves 3 to 4 inches apart (and at least 3 inches from the oven wall) so that the air can flow freely between and around them. A sheet cake pan should be set in the center of the oven rack. Place two layer cake pans on a single shelf several inches apart; divide three layer cake pans between the upper and lower level racks, two on one rack and the third in the center of the second rack.

Fully baked layer cakes and sheet cakes are well risen, and the sides will pull away ever so slightly from the edges of the baking pan(s). The shrinkage from the sides is a handy, sure sign that the cake is baked. A wooden pick inserted 1 inch from the center will be withdrawn without a wet strip of uncooked batter or many wet, clinging crumbs. A few somewhat moist (not damp) crumbs that might appear on the pick are acceptable and really incidental; this is not a sign that the cake is underbaked. Occasionally, cakes rich in chocolate will behave in this way when tested. Also, a wooden pick used to test any cakes that include chocolate chips (or fresh berries, such as blueberries or raspberries) will emerge with a small wisp of melted chocolate (or fruit juice) adhering to it; this is to be expected and, again, is not an indication that the cake is underbaked.

Another conventional method for determining the stage at which a cake is fully baked is to lightly depress the surface to see if it rises up again. Is it dependable? Sometimes. The texture—or baked structure—of layer cakes and sheet cakes varies to the extent that some completely baked cakes will lightly "bounce" to the touch of a finger, while others will have very little spring and still be baked through. For example, cakes boosted with both beaten egg whites and baking powder will spring back more decisively than others, while some chocolate cakes, made with plenty of melted chocolate, may not distinctly spring back to the touch but will still be thoroughly baked.

Basically, the combined visual test of checking the sides of the pan for retraction and considerately poking the inside of the cake with a toothpick is the best examination of doneness.

One interesting note: Some seasoned bakers, I'm told, can actually *hear* an underbaked cake, explaining that such a cake "sings," or emits a high-pitched baking noise, and that a fully baked cake is rather quiet.

COOLING BAKED LAYER CAKE AND SHEET CAKES

Cool all cakes in their pans on metal racks designed for this purpose. Cake racks lift baking pans in order to allow even and thorough air circulation. Cool individual cake layers in their pans for 3 to 5 minutes, then invert onto extra racks. Carefully lift off each cake pan. Sometimes the wax paper liner will adhere to the cake layer (if so, just strip it away) and, at other times, will remain in the bottom of the cake pan. Occasionally, the grids on some cooling racks will pull away a bit of the outside of the cake layer, an aesthetic annoyance that goes unnoticed once the layers are covered with frosting. If this bothers you at all, reinvert the layers onto extra racks several more times during the cooling process to prevent sticking, or mist the cooling racks with the lightest haze (and no more) of nonstick cookware spray before inverting the cakes onto them.

Occasionally, if the oven heat is uneven, the edges of the layers may become lightly crusty. If this happens, carefully trim off the crusty part with a sharp paring knife while the layer is still on the cooling rack. Make sure to brush away all crumbs before frosting the cake.

For sheet cakes, completely cool the cake in the pan. Since the cake will be cut directly from the pan, it is unnecessary to unmold it first.

FROSTING BAKED AND COOLED LAYER CAKES AND SHEET CAKES

Usually, a cake is frosted or iced when thoroughly cooled, but there are exceptions, such as Alice's Chocolate Pan Cake with Chocolate Fudge Frosting on page 60. For this, a thick chocolate frosting is spread over the cake while warm; the frosting is easier to spread over the cake at this time.

For a layer cake, carefully flick away any crumbs using a very soft pastry brush. Use light strokes to avoid tearing delicate cake layers with the brush. Put four strips of wax paper on the cake plate, forming a square, then place on one layer, which will cover part of the wax paper. The strips will catch any drips or splatters of frosting. Spread a little of the frosting on top of the layer, using a small flexible palette knife. An offset knife works particularly well for this. Put on the next layer, carefully aligning it with the first layer. For a three-layer cake, frost the second layer and top with the remaining cake layer.

Spread the frosting on the top and sides of the cake. Peak and swirl the frosting attractively. Most frostings are smooth and creamy, and soft enough to apply over and about the cake without splitting or crushing the layers. Once in a while, a rich chocolate or vanilla frosting may stiffen up slightly, even in the brief time between making the frosting and assembling the cake. If this happens, beat a little milk (1 teaspoon at a time) into the frosting until it is easy enough to spread. After about 1 hour, it is safe to gently tug at each wax paper strip and glide it away from the bottom of the cake.

For a sheet cake, spread the frosting on top of the cake, taking care to keep it neatly within the edges of the cake pan. Smooth the frosting attractively over the top. Depending upon the type of cake, you can decorate the top of the frosted sheet cake with chopped nuts, shaved chocolate, or flaked coconut.

5

Layer Cakes

Years ago, a standard fixture on the American kitchen countertop was a metal or glass cake keeper that secured some kind of delectable layer cake, pound cake, or coffee cake. During my childhood days, a pressed-glass dome typically accommodated a tweedy chocolate layer cake (known as My Mother's Speckled Chocolate Cake and detailed on page 24) or a deep, dark chocolate cake such as the Wellesley Fudge Cake described on page 46. A layer cake was always one of my favorite desserts, and one or another of my mother's cakes are remembered still by friends.

What keeps a splendid layer cake in my memory is its soft texture and tender lightness. The velvety grain of the cake and the creaminess of a good homemade frosting is a combination that has endured over time and, now and then, even withstands an occasional reinvention. Layer cakes are at their ideal peak of flavor and texture if served within 6 to 8 hours of baking and assembling. But an airtight container, specifically designed to hold cakes up to 3 layers tall, is the best way to preserve—for 1 or 2 days—the goodness of any of the layer cakes in this chapter. If the cake is made in advance of serving, assemble it directly on the base of the storage container, rather than composing the cake on a plate or platter and attempting to transfer it to the storage container.

Home-Style Chocolate Cake

One 2-layer, 9-inch cake, serving 12 to 16

As a basic chocolate layer cake, this simple version has a straightforward chocolate flavor and light texture. Its goodness relies only on modest pantry staples and refrigerated dairy ingredients. The cake uses whole milk as the liquid element, although half-and-half can be substituted for a slightly richer taste. Its old-fashioned excellence makes this cake perfect to serve at an informal dinner or Sunday supper.

1½ cups unsifted *all-purpose flour*
½ cup unsifted *cake flour*
2½ teaspoons baking powder
½ teaspoon salt
8 tablespoons (1 stick) unsalted butter, softened
3 tablespoons solid shortening
1½ cups granulated sugar
3 extra-large eggs
3 squares (3 ounces) unsweetened chocolate, melted and cooled
2 teaspoons vanilla extract
¾ cup milk (or substitute half-and-half)

TO FINISH THE CAKE:
Wellesley Fudge Frosting (page 93), or
Sour Cream Chocolate Frosting 209½ (page 98), or
Full of Chocolate Frosting (page 95), or
Creamy Coffee Frosting (page 106)

Preheat the oven to 350 degrees. Lightly smear solid shortening inside two 9-inch layer cake pans. Line the bottom of each pan with a circle of wax paper and dust the sides with a little all-purpose flour.

Sift together the all-purpose flour, cake flour, baking powder, and salt.

Cream the butter and shortening in the large bowl of an electric mixer on moderate speed for 3 to 5 minutes. Add the granulated sugar in three additions, beating well after each portion is added. Beat on moderately high speed for 4 to 5 minutes. Blend in the eggs, one at a time, beating well after each addition. Blend in the chocolate and vanilla extract, mixing until the chocolate is thoroughly combined in the batter. Scrape down the sides of the mixing bowl frequently with a rubber spatula to keep the batter even-textured.

On low speed, alternately add the sifted mixture in three additions with the milk (or half-and-half) in two additions, beginning and ending with the sifted mixture. The batter will be medium-thick.

Pour and scrape the batter into the pans, dividing it evenly between them.

Bake the layers for 25 to 30 minutes, or until a wooden pick inserted into the center of each layer is withdrawn without any wet, clinging particles. The fully baked layers will pull away slightly from the sides of the pan.

Cool each layer in the pan on a rack for 5 minutes. Carefully invert each layer onto a cooling rack, peel away the wax paper if it clings to the cake, and invert again to cool right-side-up.

Assemble the cake with the frosting, spreading it between each layer, and over and about the sides and top of the cake.

My Mother's Speckled Chocolate Cake

One 2-layer, 9-inch cake, serving 12 to 16

This was one of my mother's favorite layer cakes, which secured her reputation as a skilled avocational baker. The layers have a tweedlike appearance and are covered with a thin chocolate icing that gets spooned and spread over the baked layers. It was this thin, glazelike icing that traditionally covered the soft, delicate layers, but you could also choose one of the thicker, creamier chocolate frostings in this book.

The chocolate blended into the cake batter, which gives the cake its speckled appearance, is grated on the fine holes of a hand grater or in a rotary grater (used for reducing Parmesan cheese to fine, fine threads). Years ago, my mother used squares of semisweet chocolate (individually wrapped 1-ounce squares are packaged eight to the box); I sometimes replace the semisweet chocolate with bittersweet bar chocolate. No matter what kind of chocolate you use, be sure to grate it onto a large sheet of wax paper or onto a wide plate, for the chocolate tends to "fly away" as it is prepared. And remember that finely grated chocolate melts readily even if exposed to the warmth of the palm of your hand, so handle it carefully and grate it in the coolest part of your kitchen.

2¼ cups unsifted *cake flour*
3 teaspoons baking powder
¼ teaspoon salt
8 tablespoons (1 stick) unsalted butter, softened
1⅓ cups granulated sugar
3 extra-large eggs, separated
1 teaspoon vanilla extract
1 cup milk
2 ounces (2 squares) semisweet chocolate or *2 ounces (two-thirds of a 3-ounce bar) bittersweet bar chocolate (such as Lindt Excellence or Tobler Tradition), grated on the fine holes of a hand grater, or in a rotary grater*
Pinch of cream of tartar

TO FINISH THE CAKE:

My Mother's Thin and Rich Chocolate Icing (page 94), or
Full of Chocolate Frosting (page 95), or
Butter and Cream Chocolate Frosting (page 99), or
Soft Chocolate Frosting (page 97)

Preheat the oven to 350 degrees. Lightly smear solid shortening inside two 9-inch layer cake pans. Line the bottom of each pan with a circle of wax paper and dust the sides with a little all-purpose flour.

Sift the cake flour, baking powder, and salt twice.

Cream the butter in the large bowl of an electric mixer on moderate speed for 3 to 4 minutes. Add 1 cup granulated sugar in two additions, beating well after each portion is added. Beat on moderately high speed for 3 minutes. Blend in the egg yolks, one at a time, beating well after each addition. Blend in the vanilla extract. Scrape down the sides of the mixing bowl frequently with a rubber spatula to keep the batter even-textured.

On low speed, alternately add the sifted mixture in three additions with the milk in two additions, beginning and ending with the sifted mixture. Stir in the grated chocolate.

Beat the egg whites in a clean, dry mixing bowl at moderately high speed until soft peaks are formed. Add a pinch of cream of tartar and beat for 10 seconds. Add the remaining granulated sugar by tablespoons, beating for about 30 seconds (or until incorporated) before adding the next tablespoon. The whites should be glossy, firm (but not stiff), smooth, and moist-looking.

Stir about ½ cup of the beaten whites into the batter to lighten it. Fold in the remaining whites. Very small, stray patches or slivers of the whites will probably remain in the batter, which is fine.

Spoon the batter into the pans, dividing it evenly between them.

Bake the layers for 30 minutes, or until a wooden pick inserted into the center of each layer is withdrawn without any clinging particles. The fully baked layers will pull away slightly from the sides of the pan.

Cool each layer in the pan on a rack for 5 minutes. Carefully invert each layer onto a cooling rack, peel away the wax paper if it clings to the cake, and invert again to cool right-side-up.

Assemble the cake with My Mother's Thin and Rich Chocolate Icing, spooning and spreading it (the consistency is somewhat thin and runny) between each layer and over the top and sides of the cake.

Traditional Golden Cake

One 2-layer, 9-inch cake, serving 12 to 16

This soft-textured cake is plain and simply flavored.

2 cups sifted *all-purpose flour*
¼ cup sifted *cake flour*
2¼ teaspoons baking powder
¼ teaspoon salt
7 tablespoons (1 stick less *1 tablespoon) unsalted butter, softened*
4 tablespoons solid shortening
1½ cups granulated sugar
3 extra-large eggs
1½ teaspoons vanilla extract
¼ teaspoon almond extract
1 cup milk

TO FINISH THE CAKE:
Wellesley Fudge Frosting (page 93), or
Sour Cream Chocolate Frosting 209½ (page 98), or
Full of Chocolate Frosting (page 95), or
Soft Chocolate Frosting (page 97)

Preheat the oven to 350 degrees. Lightly smear solid shortening inside two 9-inch layer cake pans. Line the bottom of each pan with a circle of wax paper and dust the sides with a little all-purpose flour.

Resift the all-purpose flour and cake flour with the baking powder and salt.

Cream the butter and shortening in the large bowl of an electric mixer on moderate speed for 4 minutes. Add the granulated sugar in three additions, beating well after each portion is added. Beat on moderately high speed for 4 minutes. Blend in the eggs, one at a time, beating well after each addition. Blend in the vanilla extract and almond extract. Scrape down the sides of the mixing bowl frequently with a rubber spatula to keep the batter even-textured.

On low speed, alternately add the sifted mixture in three additions with the milk in two additions, beginning and ending with the sifted mixture.

Spoon the batter into the pans, dividing it evenly between them.

Bake the layers for 25 minutes, or until a wooden pick inserted into the center of each layer is withdrawn without any wet, clinging particles. The fully baked layers will pull away slightly from the sides of the pan.

Cool each layer in the pan on a rack for 5 minutes. Carefully invert each layer onto a cooling rack, peel away the wax paper if it clings to the cake, and invert again to cool right-side-up.

Assemble the cake with the frosting, spreading it between each layer, and over and about the sides and top of the cake.

Buttercrunch Cake

One 2-layer, 9-inch cake, serving 12 to 16

Bits of chopped toffee candy appear as crunchy-chewy specks in soft layers of yellow cake. Pairing the cake layers with a chocolate frosting accents the flavor of the chocolate candy.

2¼ *cups* sifted *cake flour*
2 *teaspoons baking powder*
½ *teaspoon salt*
¼ *teaspoon freshly grated nutmeg*
3 *bars (1.4 ounces each) chocolate-covered almond toffee candy, chopped*
6 *tablespoons (¾ stick) unsalted butter, softened*
3 *tablespoons solid shortening*
1½ *cups granulated sugar*
2 *extra-large eggs*
1½ *teaspoons vanilla extract*
½ *teaspoon almond extract*
1 *cup milk*

TO FINISH THE CAKE:
Butter and Cream Chocolate Frosting (page 99), or
Wellesley Fudge Frosting (page 93), or
Full of Chocolate Frosting (page 95)

Preheat the oven to 350 degrees. Lightly smear solid shortening inside two 9-inch layer cake pans. Line the bottom of each pan with a circle of wax paper and dust the sides with a little all-purpose flour.

Resift the cake flour with the baking powder, salt, and nutmeg. Toss the toffee candy with 1½ teaspoons of the sifted mixture.

Cream the butter and shortening in the large bowl of an electric mixer on moderate speed for 3 to 4 minutes. Add the granulated sugar in three additions, beating well after each portion is added. Beat on moderately high speed for 3 minutes. Blend in the eggs, one at a time, beating well after each addition. Blend in the vanilla extract and almond extract. Scrape down the sides of the mixing bowl frequently with a rubber spatula to keep the batter even-textured.

On low speed, alternately add the sifted mixture in three additions with the milk in two additions, beginning and ending with the sifted mixture. Stir in the toffee candy.

Spoon the batter into the pans, dividing it evenly between them.

Bake the layers for 25 to 30 minutes, or until a wooden pick inserted into the center of each layer is withdrawn without any wet, clinging particles. The fully baked layers will pull away slightly from the sides of the pan.

Cool each layer in the pan on a rack for 5 minutes. Carefully invert each layer onto a cooling rack, peel away the wax paper if it clings to the cake, and invert again to cool right-side-up.

Assemble the cake with the frosting, spreading it between each layer, and over and about the sides and top of the cake.

Sour Cream Chocolate Cake 209½

One 3-layer, 8-inch cake, serving 12

Situated neatly in the Capitol Hill section of Washington, D.C., 209½ was a much-beloved restaurant that flourished from 1977 to 1987 under the watchful eyes of proprietors Jason Wolin, Joel Wolin, and Rochelle Rose. The brothers Jason and Joel baked this enormously popular cake daily for years, and shared the recipe for this deluxe treat with me. (Rochelle Rose, the mother of Jason and Joel, is also a superb baker.)

According to Jason Wolin, "the cake is an adaptation of Maida Heatter's Sour Cream Chocolate Layer Cake," published in *Maida Heatter's Book of Great Desserts* (New York: Alfred A. Knopf, 1974); Wolin uses more butter, chocolate, and vanilla extract, replaces the light brown sugar with the dark brown variety, and bakes the cake in three 8-inch cake pans. He favors serving the cake about 12 hours after it is baked, but I find it difficult to wait that long.

Surely this is a cake for celebrations and weekend dinners, and for the time when nothing else but the opulent flavor of chocolate will do. The frosting that partners this cake, Jason's Sour Cream Chocolate Frosting 209½, is light and quite creamy, and so very good that you'd be inclined to use it with nearly any of the chocolate, white, or yellow cakes in this book. I love to work with it, for it's the type of frosting that can be spread over and over again without losing a bit of its soft and glimmering texture.

5 squares (5 ounces) unsweetened chocolate, roughly chopped
½ cup boiling water
2 cups sifted cake flour
1½ teaspoons baking powder
1 teaspoon baking soda
¼ teaspoon salt
16 tablespoons (2 sticks) unsalted butter, softened
1 cup granulated sugar
⅔ cup firmly packed dark brown sugar
3 extra-large eggs
1 tablespoon vanilla extract
1 cup sour cream

TO FINISH THE CAKE:
Sour Cream Chocolate Frosting 209½ (page 98)

Preheat the oven to 375 degrees. Lightly smear solid shortening inside three 8-inch layer cake pans. Line the bottom of each pan with a circle of wax paper and dust the sides with a little all-purpose flour.

Place the chocolate in a heatproof bowl, add the boiling water, and let stand until the chocolate is melted completely, about 15 minutes, stirring from time to time.

Resift the cake flour with the baking powder, baking soda, and salt.

Cream the butter in the large bowl of an electric mixer on moderate speed for 3 to 4 minutes. Add the granulated sugar in two additions, beating well after each portion is added. Add the brown sugar and continue beating on moderately high speed for 3 minutes. Blend in the eggs, one at a time, beating well after each addition. Beat in the vanilla extract. Scrape down the sides of the mixing bowl frequently with a rubber spatula to keep the batter even-textured.

On low speed, alternately add the sifted mixture in three additions with the sour cream in two additions, beginning and ending with the sifted mixture.

Pour and scrape the batter into the pans, dividing it evenly among them.

Bake the layers for 30 minutes, or until a wooden pick inserted into the center of each layer is withdrawn without any wet, clinging particles. The fully baked layers will pull away slightly from the sides of the pan.

Cool each layer in the pan on a rack for 5 minutes. Carefully invert each layer onto a cooling rack, peel away the wax paper if it clings to the cake, and invert again to cool right-side-up.

Assemble the cake with the Sour Cream Chocolate Frosting 209½, spreading it between each layer, and over and about the sides and top of the cake.

German Sweet Chocolate Cake

One 3-layer, 9-inch cake, serving 16

The recipe for this traditional layer cake was passed down to me many years ago by my mother, a recipe that she presumably clipped from the label of the sweet chocolate named Baker's German's Sweet Chocolate Bar, or she received it from a group of friends who routinely swapped cake recipes. The layers are supple and tender, and the frosting, applied between the layers and to the top of the cake is rich, sweet, and candylike. And like so many cakes made famous by the use of specific ingredients (including the Wellesley Fudge Cake on page 46), many variations of this cake (and its accompanying frosting) have surfaced over the years. This one is made with cake flour, while other recipes have surfaced that use all-purpose flour in a 2-cup measurement.

1 package (4 ounces) Baker's German's Sweet Chocolate Bar, coarsely chopped
½ cup boiling water
2¼ cups unsifted *cake flour*
1 teaspoon baking soda
½ teaspoon salt
16 tablespoons (2 sticks) unsalted butter, softened
2 cups granulated sugar
4 extra-large eggs, separated
1 teaspoon vanilla extract
1 cup buttermilk

TO FINISH THE CAKE:
Coconut-Pecan Frosting (page 100)

Preheat the oven to 350 degrees. Lightly smear solid shortening inside three 9-inch layer cake pans. Line the bottom of each pan with a circle of wax paper and dust the sides with a little all-purpose flour.

Combine the chocolate and boiling water in a heatproof bowl and let stand, stirring occasionally, until the chocolate is melted.

Sift the cake flour with the baking soda and salt.

Cream the butter in the large bowl of an electric mixer on moderate speed for 4 to 5 minutes. Add the granulated sugar in three additions, beating well after each portion is added. Beat on moderately high speed for 3 minutes. Blend in the egg yolks, one at a time, beating well after each addition. Blend in the vanilla extract. Scrape down the sides of the mixing bowl frequently with a rubber spatula to keep the batter even-textured. Whisk the chocolate and water mixture to blend it completely, then beat it into the batter, using moderately low speed.

On low speed, alternately add the sifted mixture in three additions with the buttermilk in two additions, beginning and ending with the sifted mixture.

Beat the egg whites in a clean, dry bowl until they begin to foam, then continue beating until firm (not stiff) peaks are formed. Stir about one quarter of the whites into the batter, then fold in the remaining whites until any large patches disappear.

Spoon the batter into the pans, dividing it evenly among them.

Bake the layers for 30 to 35 minutes, or until a wooden pick inserted into the center of each layer is withdrawn without any wet, clinging particles. The fully baked layers will pull away slightly from the sides of the pan.

Cool each layer in the pan on a rack for 5 minutes. Carefully invert each layer onto a cooling rack, peel away the wax paper if it clings to the cake, and invert again to cool right-side-up.

Assemble the cake with the Coconut-Pecan Frosting, spreading it between each layer, and over the top of the cake.

Marble Cake

One 2-layer, 10-inch cake, serving 16

Patches of a moist chocolate and vanilla batter, run together slightly with the tip of a table knife, produce cake layers with a handsome baked pattern. To achieve the proper mingling of batters, all you need to do is blend half of the vanilla-flavored batter with a mixture of melted, unsweetened chocolate and a dash of baking soda, spoon dollops of that batter over the vanilla batter, and swirl the two together.

2 cups sifted *cake flour*
2½ teaspoons baking powder
¼ teaspoon salt
6 tablespoons (¾ stick) unsalted butter, softened
5 tablespoons solid shortening
1½ cups granulated sugar
3 extra-large eggs
2 teaspoons vanilla extract
½ teaspoon almond extract
¾ cup milk (or half-and-half)
3 squares (3 ounces) unsweetened chocolate, melted and cooled
⅛ teaspoon baking soda

TO FINISH THE CAKE:
Wellesley Fudge Frosting (page 93), or
Full of Chocolate Frosting (page 95), or
Sour Cream Chocolate Frosting 209½ (page 98), or
My Mother's Thin and Rich Chocolate Icing (page 94), or
Butter and Cream Chocolate Frosting (page 99)

Preheat the oven to 350 degrees. Lightly smear solid shortening inside two 10-inch layer cake pans. Line the bottom of each pan with a circle of wax paper and dust the sides with a little all-purpose flour.

Resift the cake flour with the baking powder and salt.

Cream the butter and shortening in the large bowl of an electric mixer on moderate speed for 3 to 4 minutes. Add the granulated sugar in three additions, beating well after each portion is added. Beat on moderately high speed for 3 minutes. Blend in the eggs, one at a time, beating well after each addition. Blend in the vanilla extract and almond extract. Scrape down the sides of the mixing bowl frequently with a rubber spatula to keep the batter even-textured.

On low speed, alternately add the sifted mixture in three additions with the milk (or half-and-half) in two additions, beginning and ending with the sifted mixture.

Combine the melted chocolate and baking soda.

Spoon half of the vanilla batter into the pans, dividing it evenly between them. Beat the melted chocolate–baking soda mixture into the remaining vanilla batter; the chocolate batter will be somewhat thicker. Drop dollops of the chocolate batter on top of the vanilla batter, placing about eight mounds of batter in each baking pan. Using a round-bladed table knife or a thin palette knife, swirl the chocolate batter through the vanilla batter.

Shake each pan gently from side to side to level the top layer of batter.

Bake the layers for 25 to 30 minutes, or until a wooden pick inserted into the center of each layer is withdrawn without any wet, clinging particles. The fully baked layers will pull away slightly from the sides of the pan.

Cool each layer in the pan on a rack for 5 minutes. Carefully invert each layer onto a cooling rack, peel away the wax paper if it clings to the cake, and invert again to cool right-side-up.

Assemble the cake with the frosting, spreading it between each layer, and over and about the sides and top of the cake.

Old-Fashioned Light Chocolate Cake

One 2-layer, 10-inch cake, serving 12 to 16

With its satisfying chocolate flavor and tender texture, this is a good, fundamental layer cake that is pleasing with almost any kind of frosting or icing, in particular, the Wellesley Fudge Frosting or the Soft Chocolate Frosting.

2¼ cups sifted *cake flour*
¾ teaspoon baking soda
¼ teaspoon salt
7 tablespoons (1 stick less *1 tablespoon) unsalted butter, softened*
4 tablespoons solid shortening
1⅔ cups superfine sugar
3 extra-large eggs
1½ teaspoons vanilla extract
3 squares (3 ounces) unsweetened chocolate, melted and cooled
1 cup milk blended with *1 tablespoon lemon juice*

TO FINISH THE CAKE:
Wellesley Fudge Frosting (page 93), or
Soft Chocolate Frosting (page 97), or
Sour Cream Chocolate Frosting 209½ (page 98), or
My Mother's Thin and Rich Chocolate Icing (page 94), or
Butter and Cream Chocolate Frosting (page 99), or
Creamy Coffee Frosting (page 106)

Preheat the oven to 350 degrees. Lightly smear solid shortening inside two 10-inch layer cake pans. Line the bottom of each pan with a circle of wax paper and dust the sides with a little all-purpose flour.

Resift the cake flour with the baking soda and salt.

Cream the butter and shortening in the large bowl of an electric mixer on moderate speed for 2 minutes. Add the superfine sugar in three additions, beating well after each portion is added. Beat on moderately high speed for

1 minute. Blend in the eggs, one at a time, beating well after each addition. Blend in the vanilla extract and melted chocolate. Scrape down the sides of the mixing bowl frequently with a rubber spatula to keep the batter even-textured.

On low speed, alternately add the sifted mixture in three additions with the milk in two additions, beginning and ending with the sifted mixture. The batter will be soft, spoonable, and fluffy-creamy, almost like a light buttercream.

Spoon the batter into the pans, dividing it evenly between them.

Bake the layers for 30 to 35 minutes, or until a wooden pick inserted into the center of each layer is withdrawn without any wet, clinging particles. The fully baked layers will pull away slightly from the sides of the pan.

Cool each layer in the pan on a rack for 5 minutes. Carefully invert each layer onto a cooling rack, peel away the wax paper if it clings to the cake, and invert again to cool right-side-up.

Assemble the cake with the frosting, spreading it between each layer, and over and about the sides and top of the cake.

Birthday Buttermilk Chocolate Cake

One 2-layer, 9-inch cake, serving 12 to 16

Feathery and luscious, with a clear chocolate flavor, this is a crowd-pleasing layer cake, good enough to be served at birthdays and other such celebrations. The buttermilk in the batter acts as a tenderizing agent, and contributes to its fine texture.

2¼ cups sifted *all-purpose flour*
1 teaspoon baking soda
½ teaspoon salt
6 tablespoons (¾ stick) unsalted butter, softened
5 tablespoons solid shortening
1½ cups granulated sugar
2 extra-large eggs
2 extra-large egg yolks
2 teaspoons vanilla extract
3 squares (3 ounces) unsweetened chocolate, melted and cooled
1⅛ cups (1 cup plus *2 tablespoons) buttermilk*

TO FINISH THE CAKE:
Wellesley Fudge Frosting (page 93), or
Full of Chocolate Frosting (page 95), or
Sour Cream Chocolate Frosting 209½ (page 98), or
Butter and Cream Chocolate Frosting (page 99), or
Creamy Coffee Frosting (page 106)

Preheat the oven to 350 degrees. Lightly smear solid shortening inside two 9-inch layer cake pans. Line the bottom of each pan with a circle of wax paper and dust the sides with a little all-purpose flour.

Resift the all-purpose flour with the baking soda and salt.

Cream the butter and shortening in the large bowl of an electric mixer on moderate speed for 3 minutes. Add the granulated sugar in three additions, beating well after each portion is added. Beat on moderately high speed for 4 minutes. Blend in the eggs, one at a time, beating well after each addition. Blend in the egg yolks. Add the vanilla extract and chocolate, mixing until the chocolate colors the batter completely. Scrape down the sides of the mixing bowl frequently with a rubber spatula to keep the batter even-textured.

On low speed, alternately add the sifted mixture in three additions with the buttermilk in two additions, beginning and ending with the sifted mixture.

Pour and scrape the batter into the pans, dividing it evenly between them.

Bake the layers for 25 to 30 minutes, or until a wooden pick inserted into the center of each layer is withdrawn without any wet, clinging particles. The fully baked layers will pull away slightly from the sides of the pan.

Cool each layer in the pan on a rack for 5 minutes. Carefully invert each layer onto a cooling rack, peel away the wax paper if it clings to the cake, and invert again to cool right-side-up.

Assemble the cake with the frosting, spreading it between each layer, and over and about the sides and top of the cake.

A Light White Cake

One 3-layer, 9-inch cake, serving 16

The recipe for this exceedingly tender and cushiony cake has been in my files for years, and although I have made several changes in its structure, including the type and amount of fat and flour, the key liquid ingredient has remained the same—a full 1½ cups of ice water. For that (and to guarantee the success of the recipe), you must use *icy* cold water, not merely cold tap water: To do this, load a big measuring cup with cold water and ice cubes, then remove the ice and carefully measure the water right before adding it to the batter.

The primary flavoring in this cake recipe as it was passed down to me was coconut—a brimming 1⅓ cups of sweetened flaked coconut accented the batter. That recipe has been modified to create a plain vanilla cake, one that is so good with waves of chocolate frosting. The coconut variation appears below, but you should really bake the plain version first and see how wonderful a white cake can be.

2¼ cups unsifted *cake flour*
¾ cup unsifted *all-purpose flour*
3 teaspoons baking powder
¼ teaspoon baking soda
¾ teaspoon salt
¼ teaspoon freshly grated nutmeg
8 tablespoons (1 stick) unsalted butter, softened
4 tablespoons solid shortening
2 cups plus *2 tablespoons superfine sugar*
2½ teaspoons vanilla extract
Seed scrapings from the inside of ½ vanilla bean (optional)
1½ cups ice-cold water
4 extra-large egg whites
⅛ teaspoon cream of tartar

TO FINISH THE CAKE:

Wellesley Fudge Frosting (page 93), or
Full of Chocolate Frosting (page 95), or
Sour Cream Chocolate Frosting 209½ *(page 98)*

Preheat the oven to 350 degrees. Lightly smear solid shortening inside three 9-inch layer cake pans. Line the bottom of each pan with a circle of wax paper and dust the sides with a little all-purpose flour.

Sift the cake flour, all-purpose flour, baking powder, baking soda, salt, and nutmeg two times.

Cream the butter and shortening in the large bowl of an electric mixer on moderate speed for 3 to 4 minutes. Add the 2 cups of superfine sugar in five additions, beating well after each portion is added. Beat on moderately high speed for 4 to 5 minutes, or until the mixture looks nicely whipped and almost white in color. Blend in the vanilla extract and the vanilla bean scrapings, if you are using them. Scrape down the sides of the mixing bowl frequently with a rubber spatula to keep the batter even-textured.

On low speed, alternately add the sifted mixture in three additions with the ice-cold water in two additions, beginning and ending with the sifted mixture. The batter will resemble thick buttercream.

Beat the egg whites in a clean, dry bowl until they begin to foam, add the cream of tartar, and continue beating until soft peaks are formed. Sprinkle over the remaining 2 tablespoons of superfine sugar and continue beating until firm (not stiff) peaks are formed. Vigorously stir about one quarter of the whites into the batter, then fold in the remaining whites until all stray patches disappear.

Spoon the batter into the pans, dividing it evenly among them.

Bake the layers for 25 to 30 minutes, or until a wooden pick inserted into the center of each layer is withdrawn without any wet, clinging particles. The fully baked layers will pull away from the sides of the pan and the top will be a mottled pale golden color.

Cool each layer in the pan on a rack for 3 to 5 minutes. Carefully invert each layer onto a cooling rack, peel away the wax paper if it clings to the cake, and invert again to cool right-side-up.

Assemble the cake with the frosting, spreading it between each layer, and over and about the sides and top of the cake.

VARIATION

For *A Light White Coconut Cake*, mix 1⅓ cups sweetened flaked coconut into the batter before you add the egg whites. For the frosting, use either the Vanilla Butter Frosting (page 101) or Fluffy White Frosting (page 104).

Banana Cake

One 2-layer, 10-inch cake, serving 16

For years I have been in search of a good, packed-with-taste banana layer cake—light and soft-textured, made with all the usual pantry staples. While a banana tea bread (or loaf cake) or batch of muffins can have an appealing dense "crumb," a layer cake made with the fruit should, be especially delicate.

To achieve that state, I use cake flour, a combination of leavenings, a mixture of two fats (butter and solid shortening), and buttermilk. The butter is used for flavor, while the shortening gives the cake its proper volume. This formula is the one I have settled upon, and it will delight those who like a cake that is at once fruity, rich, and satisfying.

2½ cups sifted *cake flour*
1¼ teaspoons baking powder
1 teaspoon baking soda
½ teaspoon salt
8 tablespoons (1 stick) unsalted butter, softened
4 tablespoons solid shortening
1½ cups plus *2 tablespoons granulated sugar*
2 extra-large eggs
2 teaspoons vanilla extract
1⅓ cups mashed, ripe bananas (about 3 small bananas)
½ cup plus *1 tablespoon buttermilk*

TO FINISH THE CAKE:
Butter and Cream Chocolate Frosting (page 99), or
Sour Cream Chocolate Frosting 209½ (page 98), or
Brown Sugar Butter Frosting (page 102), or
Wellesley Fudge Frosting (page 93), or
Full of Chocolate Frosting (page 95)

Preheat the oven to 350 degrees. Lightly smear solid shortening inside two 10-inch layer cake pans. Line the bottom of each pan with a circle of wax paper and dust the sides with a little all-purpose flour.

Resift the cake flour with the baking powder, baking soda, and salt.

Cream the butter and shortening in the large bowl of an electric mixer on moderate speed for 3 to 4 minutes. Add the granulated sugar in three additions, beating well after each portion is added. Beat on moderately high speed for 3 minutes. Blend in the eggs, one at a time, beating well after each addition. Blend in the vanilla extract and mashed bananas. Scrape down the sides of the mixing bowl frequently with a rubber spatula to keep the batter even-textured.

On low speed, alternately add the sifted mixture in three additions with the buttermilk in two additions, beginning and ending with the sifted mixture.

Pour and scrape the batter into the pans, dividing it evenly between them.

Bake the layers for 30 minutes, or until a wooden pick inserted into the center of each layer is withdrawn without any wet, clinging particles. The fully baked layers will pull away slightly from the sides of the pan.

Cool each layer in the pan on a rack for 5 minutes. Carefully invert each layer onto a cooling rack, peel away the wax paper if it clings to the cake, and invert again to cool right-side-up.

Assemble the cake with the frosting, spreading it between each layer, and over and about the sides and top of the cake.

VARIATIONS

For *Banana Cake with Chocolate Chips*, toss ½ cup miniature semisweet chocolate chips with 2 teaspoons of the sifted flour mixture. Stir the chocolate chips into the batter after the last portion of flour has been added. Use any of the frostings suggested in the recipe *except* the Brown Sugar Butter Frosting.

For *Banana Cake with Grated Chocolate*, grate 2 squares (2 ounces) semisweet chocolate on the fine holes of a hand grater, or in the container of a small rotary drum grater. Stir the chocolate into the batter after the last portion of flour has been added. Use any of the frostings suggested in the recipe *except* the Brown Sugar Butter Frosting.

For *Banana Cake with Sliced Banana Filling*, peel and slice a ripe banana. Arrange the banana slices over the top of the first frosted cake layer, top with the second layer, then frost the entire cake. Use any of the frostings suggested in the recipe.

Wellesley Fudge Cake

One 2-layer, 9-inch cake, serving 12 to 16

The fudge cake you have here is quite dark in color and fairly light in texture. The baked layers are slathered in Wellesley Fudge Frosting, and this rich and chocolaty finish is what adds to the character of the cake.

The cake is traditionally made with Baker's unsweetened chocolate and Swan's Down cake flour, and the frosting with Baker's unsweetened chocolate, which, to say the least, established its reputation. Sometimes the recipe was printed in magazine advertisements for those ingredients, or on the side or back panel of the box of cake flour, or directly on (or inside) the box of baking chocolate. My mother clipped and used this recipe, but there are many other recipes for this kind of cake in existence and the recipe has been altered a bit here and there, depending upon where it was printed.

As a birthday cake (served plain, with scoops of vanilla ice cream or with lightly whipped cream) it's peerless and deserves to be passed along to the next generation of bakers.

4 squares (4 ounces) unsweetened chocolate
½ cup hot water
½ cup plus *1¼ cups granulated sugar*
1 teaspoon vanilla extract
2 cups sifted *cake flour*
1 teaspoon baking soda
½ teaspoon salt (see Ingredient Note below)
8 tablespoons (1 stick) unsalted butter, softened
3 extra-large eggs
¾ cup milk

TO FINISH THE CAKE:
Wellesley Fudge Frosting (page 93)

Preheat the oven to 350 degrees. Lightly smear solid shortening inside two 9-inch layer cake pans. Line the bottom of each pan with a circle of wax paper and dust the sides with a little all-purpose flour.

Place the chocolate and hot water in a heavy saucepan, set over low heat, and cook until the chocolate is melted and smooth, stirring now and then. Add the ½ cup granulated sugar and cook for 2 minutes, stirring. Cool the mixture to lukewarm, then add the vanilla extract.

Resift the cake flour with the baking soda and salt.

Cream the butter in the large bowl of an electric mixer on moderate speed for 3 to 4 minutes. Add the remaining granulated sugar in two additions, beating well after each portion is added. Beat on moderately high speed for 3 to 4 minutes. Blend in the eggs, one at a time, beating well after each addition. Scrape down the sides of the mixing bowl frequently with a rubber spatula to keep the batter even-textured. Stir in the cooked chocolate mixture, scraping down the bowl again to blend well.

On low speed, alternately add the sifted mixture in three additions with the milk in two additions, beginning and ending with the sifted mixture.

Spoon the batter into the pans, dividing it evenly between them.

Bake the layers for 30 minutes, or until a wooden pick inserted into the center of each layer is withdrawn without any wet, clinging particles. The fully baked layers will pull away slightly from the sides of the pan.

Cool each layer in the pan on a rack for 5 minutes. Carefully invert each layer onto a cooling rack, peel away the wax paper if it clings to the cake, and invert again to cool right-side-up.

Assemble the cake with the Wellesley Fudge Frosting, spreading it between each layer, and over and about the sides and top of the cake.

INGREDIENT NOTE: Many of the recipes for Wellesley Fudge Cake that I have encountered use 1 teaspoon salt, but I prefer to use ½ teaspoon.

Coconut Cake

One 2-layer, 9-inch cake, serving 12 to 16

For coconut lovers, a classic yellow cake covered with a soft and dreamy frosting and handfuls of flaked coconut is sheer delight. This cake is light but substantial, and makes an unforgettable home-style birthday cake.

2¼ cups sifted *cake flour*
2¼ teaspoons baking powder
½ teaspoon salt
9 tablespoons (1 stick plus *1 tablespoon) unsalted butter, softened*
3 tablespoons solid shortening
1½ cups superfine sugar
2 extra-large eggs
2 extra-large egg yolks
2 teaspoons vanilla extract
¾ cup plus *2 tablespoons milk*
½ cup sweetened flaked coconut

TO FINISH THE CAKE:
Fluffy White Frosting (page 104), or *Vanilla Butter Frosting (page 101)*
About 3 cups sweetened flaked coconut

Preheat the oven to 350 degrees. Lightly smear solid shortening inside two 9-inch layer cake pans. Line the bottom of each pan with a circle of wax paper and dust the sides with a little all-purpose flour.

Resift the cake flour with the baking powder and salt twice.

Cream the butter and shortening in the large bowl of an electric mixer on moderate speed for 3 to 4 minutes. Add the superfine sugar in three additions, beating well after each portion is added. Beat on moderately high speed for 3 minutes. Blend in the eggs, one at a time, beating well after each addition. Blend in the egg yolks and vanilla extract. Scrape down the sides of the mixing bowl frequently with a rubber spatula to keep the batter even-textured.

On low speed, alternately add the sifted mixture in three additions with the milk in two additions, beginning and ending with the sifted mixture. Stir in the coconut.

Spoon the batter into the pans, dividing it evenly between them.

Bake the layers for 25 to 30 minutes, or until a wooden pick inserted into the center of each layer is withdrawn without any wet, clinging particles. The fully baked layers will pull away slightly from the sides of the pan.

Cool each layer in the pan on a rack for 5 minutes. Carefully invert each layer onto a cooling rack, peel away the wax paper if it clings to the cake, and invert again to cool right-side-up.

Assemble the cake with the frosting, spreading it between each layer, and over and about the sides and top of the cake. Carefully press the coconut around the sides and on top of the cake.

Buttery Almond Cake

One 2-layer, 10-inch cake, serving 12 to 16

Boosted with almond extract and bits of chopped almonds, this layer cake can be covered with a plain vanilla frosting or, since almonds and chocolate have a natural affinity for one another, a chocolate-based frosting. And to reinforce the almond taste further, chopped toasted almonds may be pressed onto the sides or sprinkled on the rim of the frosted cake, if you wish.

2½ cups sifted *all-purpose flour*
2¼ teaspoons baking powder
½ teaspoon salt
½ teaspoon freshly grated nutmeg
12 tablespoons (1½ sticks) unsalted butter, softened
1½ cups granulated sugar
2 extra-large egg yolks
2 extra-large eggs, separated
2½ teaspoons almond extract
¼ teaspoon vanilla extract
1 cup milk
⅔ cup chopped almonds

TO FINISH THE CAKE:
Vanilla Butter Frosting (page 101), or
Butter and Cream Chocolate Frosting (page 99), or
Sour Cream Chocolate Frosting 209½ (page 98), or
Full of Chocolate Frosting (page 95)

Preheat the oven to 350 degrees. Lightly smear solid shortening inside two 10-inch layer cake pans. Line the bottom of each pan with a circle of wax paper and dust the sides with a little all-purpose flour.

Resift the all-purpose flour with the baking powder, salt, and nutmeg.

Cream the butter in the large bowl of an electric mixer on moderate speed for 3 to 4 minutes. Add the granulated sugar in three additions, beating well after each portion is added. Beat on moderately high speed for 4 minutes.

Beat in the 4 egg yolks. Blend in the almond extract and vanilla extract. Scrape down the sides of the mixing bowl frequently with a rubber spatula to keep the batter even-textured.

On low speed, alternately add the sifted mixture in three additions with the milk in two additions, beginning and ending with the sifted mixture. Beat the 2 egg whites in a clean, dry bowl until firm (not stiff) peaks are formed. Stir about one quarter of the whites into the batter, then fold in the remaining whites. Fold in the almonds.

Spoon the batter into the pans, dividing it evenly between them.

Bake the layers for 25 to 30 minutes, or until a wooden pick inserted into the center of each layer is withdrawn without any wet, clinging particles. The fully baked layers will pull away slightly from the sides of the pan.

Cool each layer in the pan on a rack for 5 minutes. Carefully invert each layer onto a cooling rack, peel away the wax paper if it clings to the cake, and invert again to cool right-side-up.

Assemble the cake with the frosting, spreading it between each layer, and over and about the sides and top of the cake.

Golden Ginger Cake

One 2-layer, 9-inch cake, serving 12 to 16

Usually, cakes accented with ginger are darkened with molasses and brown sugar, and spiced with cinnamon, nutmeg, allspice, and cloves; this combination creates a moist, complex-tasting cake. This ginger cake, however, is made with a golden cake batter, and seasoned with minced crystallized ginger and ground ginger. Ice the cake with a slick of chocolate frosting and garnish with pieces of crystallized ginger dipped in chocolate, if you wish. This is a marvelous cake to serve at tea.

2 cups sifted *all-purpose flour*
2½ teaspoons baking powder
¼ teaspoon salt
1 teaspoon ground ginger
8 tablespoons (1 stick) unsalted butter, softened
1 cup granulated sugar
2 extra-large egg yolks
1 extra-large egg, separated
1½ teaspoons vanilla extract
¾ cup milk
⅓ cup minced crystallized ginger

TO FINISH THE CAKE:
Full of Chocolate Frosting (page 95), or
Soft Chocolate Frosting (page 97), or
Vanilla Butter Frosting (page 101)

Preheat the oven to 375 degrees. Lightly smear solid shortening inside two 9-inch layer cake pans. Line the bottom of each pan with a circle of wax paper and dust the sides with a little all-purpose flour.

Resift the all-purpose flour with the baking powder, salt, and ginger.

Cream the butter in the large bowl of an electric mixer on moderate speed for 3 minutes. Remove and reserve 2 tablespoons of the granulated sugar from the 1 cup amount, leaving ⅞ cup. Add the ⅞ cup of granulated sugar in three additions, beating well after each portion is added. Beat on moderately high speed for 3 minutes. Blend in the 3 egg yolks, beating well. Blend in the vanilla extract. Scrape down the sides of the mixing bowl frequently with a rubber spatula to keep the batter even-textured.

On low speed, alternately add the sifted mixture in three additions with the milk in two additions, beginning and ending with the sifted mixture. Beat the egg white in a clean, dry bowl until very soft peaks are formed, add the remaining 2 tablespoons of granulated sugar, and beat until firm (not stiff) peaks are formed. Fold the white into the cake batter. Stir in the minced ginger.

Spoon the batter into the pans, dividing it evenly between them.

Bake the layers for 25 minutes, or until a wooden pick inserted into the center of each layer is withdrawn without any wet, clinging particles. The fully baked layers will pull away slightly from the sides of the pan.

Cool each layer in the pan on a rack for 5 minutes. Carefully invert each layer onto a cooling rack, peel away the wax paper if it clings to the cake, and invert again to cool right-side-up.

Assemble the cake with the frosting, spreading it between each layer, and over and about the sides and top of the cake.

6

Sheet Cakes

A sheet cake is customarily baked in a 13 by 9 by 2-inch baking pan and cut into squares or rectangles for serving, although a smaller, single-layer sheet cake—more of the coffee cake or tea cake variety—can be baked in a 9 by 9 by 2-inch pan. Either way, it's an adaptable, informal kind of cake that's easy to bake and carry to an event: just transport the cake in the pan. In a graceful way, it serves a crowd with ease.

A batter intended to be baked in a sheet cake pan is entirely accommodating: it can be thick or thin, contain lots of fruit (shredded, pureed, or in the form of whole berries); suspend jagged morsels of chocolate or plenty of chopped nuts; be bulked up with rolled oats; flavored exclusively with extracts; or smoothed out with light cream or beaten egg whites. While most layer cakes are appreciated for their ethereal quality, the texture of a sheet cake can be far more variable—either fudgy, dense, fluffy, or compact.

A square of sheet cake is quite good on its own with tea or coffee, or you can build a bountiful dessert plate by accompanying the cake with other sweet accessories. Poached, sautéed, or oven-baked fruit, for example, are delicious served with Oatmeal Cake (page 68), Soft Spice Cake (page 76), or Lemon Cake (page 86), and homemade ice cream is a natural with Rich

Mocha Cake (page 84), Birthday White Cake (page 88), Alice's Chocolate Pan Cake with Chocolate Fudge Frosting (page 60), 1-2-3-4 Cake (page 57), or White Coconut and Macadamia Nut Cake (page 80).

From the standpoint of taste and texture, sheet cakes, like layer cakes, are most delectable if served within 6 to 8 hours of baking, but they, too, can be stored for a day or two longer. If you have a deep, rectangular storage container, you can place the cake in it, pan and all, and cover it without marring the surface. Alternately, an uniced sheet cake can be baked in advance, covered snugly with plastic wrap and stored at room temperature; ice or frost the cake on serving day.

1-2-3-4 Cake

One 13 by 9 by 2-inch cake, serving 16 to 20

The classic 1-2-3-4 cake is, perhaps, the matriarch of all the creamed cake batters, and should be remembered and appreciated for its simplicity and plain good taste. That nearly everyone's mother or grandmother, including mine, made the cake is enough to recommend it. (My grandmother, in her own handwriting, copied the recipe with the following title from a friend: "Trick Cake Wins Prize 1-2-3-4 Cake.")

The numerically descriptive title of the cake conveniently reflects the amount of each main ingredient used in the batter: 1 cup butter, 2 cups sugar, 3 cups flour, and 4 eggs. The amounts of other ingredients vary, such as the type and quantity of leavening and kind of liquid, and flavoring agent. The texture of the cake is soft and fine-grained. It's an ideal sheet cake to make for a birthday party because it can be covered with nearly any kind of frosting imaginable.

3 cups sifted *all-purpose flour*
3 teaspoons baking powder
½ teaspoon salt
16 tablespoons (2 sticks) unsalted butter, softened
2 cups granulated sugar
4 extra-large eggs
1 tablespoon vanilla extract
1 cup milk

TO FINISH THE CAKE:
Wellesley Fudge Frosting (page 93), or
Full of Chocolate Frosting (page 95), or
Soft Chocolate Frosting (page 97), or
Sour Cream Chocolate Frosting 209½ (page 98), or
Butter and Cream Chocolate Frosting (page 99), or
Vanilla Butter Frosting (page 101)

Preheat the oven to 375 degrees. Lightly smear solid shortening inside a 13 by 9 by 2-inch baking pan and dust with all-purpose flour.

Resift the all-purpose flour with the baking powder and salt three times.

Cream the butter in the large bowl of an electric mixer on moderate speed for 6 minutes. Add the granulated sugar in three additions, beating well after each portion is added. Beat on moderately high speed for 4 to 5 minutes, or until nearly white in color. Blend in the eggs, one at a time, beating well after each addition. Blend in the vanilla extract. Scrape down the sides of the mixing bowl frequently with a rubber spatula to keep the batter even-textured.

On low speed, alternately add the sifted mixture in three additions with the milk in two additions, beginning and ending with the sifted mixture. The batter will be medium-thick and silky-textured.

Pour and scrape the batter into the pan.

Bake the cake for 30 minutes, or until a wooden pick inserted into the center of the cake is withdrawn without any wet, clinging particles. The baked cake will pull away slightly from the sides of the pan and the top will be a medium-golden color.

Cool the cake in the pan on a rack. Cover the top of the cooled cake with the frosting. If you use any of the chocolate frostings to cover this cake, you can sprinkle the top with chopped walnuts or pecans (about 1¼ cups). And the cake, once capped with vanilla frosting, can be covered with sweetened flaked coconut (about 2 cups). For serving, cut the cake into squares.

VARIATIONS

For *Almond 1-2-3-4 Cake*, substitute almond extract for the vanilla extract. Stir ⅔ cup finely chopped almonds into the batter after the flour mixture is added.

For *1-2-3-4 Cake with Miniature Chocolate Chips*, toss ¾ cup miniature semisweet chocolate chips with 1 tablespoon of the sifted mixture. Stir the chocolate chips into the batter after the flour mixture has been added.

For *Coconut 1-2-3-4 Cake*, stir 1 cup sweetened flaked coconut into the batter after the flour mixture has been added.

Alice's Chocolate Pan Cake with Chocolate Fudge Frosting

One 13 by 9 by 2-inch cake, serving 16 to 20

Ever since I wrote *Country Cakes* (New York: Harper & Row, 1989), cooks far and wide have written me about this cake (it appears in the chapter titled "Traveling Cakes"). And now, since *Country Cakes* is part of my one-volume collection of books titled *A Country Baking Treasury* (New York: HarperCollins Publishers, 1995), the recipe is, once again, in the hands of even more chocolate fans. Bakers are devoted to this chocolate cake. The recipe comes from my friend Alice Romejko, who makes this gem for family and friends. It's a prize of a recipe and, for me, it would be unthinkable to assemble a collection of sheet cakes without including this one. So here you have it—once again.

There are two interesting aspects to the cake: the batter, ready to be poured into the baking pan, is quite thin. This is as it should be. As for frosting the cake, ignore my professional instructions to always cool a cake completely before topping it with icing or frosting. *Always* frost this cake while it is hot (within 10 minutes of removing it from the oven) or you'll be unable to spread the chocolate mixture quickly and evenly. Remarkably, the frosting sets up nicely when it is applied on the cake before it has the chance to cool down.

16 tablespoons (2 sticks) unsalted butter, cut into chunks
4 tablespoons unsifted *unsweetened cocoa*
1 cup water
2 cups granulated sugar
2 cups unsifted *cake flour*
1 teaspoon salt
½ cup buttermilk blended with *1 teaspoon baking soda*
2 extra-large eggs
1½ teaspoons vanilla extract (see Ingredient Note below)

TO FINISH THE CAKE:
Alice's Chocolate Fudge Frosting (page 96)

Preheat the oven to 400 degrees. Lightly smear solid shortening inside a 13 by 9 by 2-inch baking pan and dust with all-purpose flour.

Place the butter, cocoa, and water in a large saucepan, set over moderately high heat, and bring to the boil. Remove from the heat.

Sift the sugar, cake flour, and salt into the large bowl of an electric mixer. Whisk together the buttermilk–baking soda blend, eggs, and vanilla extract in a mixing bowl. Pour the hot butter-cocoa-water mixture over the sifted mixture and beat on moderate speed until thoroughly blended. Add the whisked egg mixture and continue beating on low speed until the batter is a uniform color, about 1½ minutes, scraping the sides of the mixing bowl as the batter is mixed. The batter will be thin.

Pour the batter into the pan.

Bake the cake for 20 to 22 minutes, or until a wooden pick inserted into the center of the cake is withdrawn without any wet, clinging particles. The baked cake will pull away slightly from the sides of the pan.

Place the cake in the pan on a rack. While it is still hot (within 10 minutes), cover the top of the cake with Alice's Chocolate Fudge Frosting. Cool the cake completely. For serving, cut the cake into squares.

INGREDIENT NOTE: Alice's recipe calls for ½ teaspoon vanilla extract, but I use an extra teaspoon of extract.

"Top Milk" Cake

One 13 by 9 by 2-inch cake, serving 16 to 20

Moist, with that light and airy texture that I love, this cake is the ideal "plain" cake meant to be served for dessert at a casual dinner, or at mid-afternoon with a hot or cold refreshment. Top milk, the richer cream that rose to the top of the glass milk jug delivered weekly (or biweekly) by dairies long ago would be, in today's culinary language, called half-and-half.

1½ cups unsifted *all-purpose flour*
½ cup unsifted *cake flour*
1 teaspoon baking soda
½ teaspoon salt
12 tablespoons (1½ sticks) unsalted butter, softened
1½ cups granulated sugar
3 extra-large eggs
2 teaspoons vanilla extract
½ teaspoon almond extract
1 cup half-and-half

TO FINISH THE CAKE:
Wellesley Fudge Frosting (page 93), or
Full of Chocolate Frosting (page 95), or
Soft Chocolate Frosting (page 97), or
Sour Cream Chocolate Frosting 209½ (page 98), or
Vanilla Butter Frosting (page 101)

Preheat the oven to 350 degrees. Lightly smear solid shortening inside a 13 by 9 by 2-inch baking pan and dust with all-purpose flour.

Sift the all-purpose flour, cake flour, baking soda, and salt.

Cream the butter in the large bowl of an electric mixer on moderate speed for 4 minutes. Add the granulated sugar in three additions, beating for 2 to 3 minutes after each portion is added. Beat on moderately high speed for

1 minute. Blend in the eggs, one at a time, beating well after each addition. Blend in the vanilla extract and almond extract. Scrape down the sides of the mixing bowl frequently with a rubber spatula to keep the batter even-textured.

On low speed, alternately add the sifted mixture in three additions with the half-and-half in two additions, beginning and ending with the sifted mixture.

Spoon the batter into the pan.

Bake the cake for 30 to 35 minutes, or until a wooden pick inserted into the center of the cake is withdrawn without any wet, clinging particles. The baked cake will pull away slightly from the sides of the pan.

Cool the cake in the pan on a rack. Cover the top of the cooled cake with the frosting. For serving, cut the cake into squares.

Spiced Carrot Cake

One 13 by 9 by 2-inch cake, serving 16 to 20

I've been making this carrot cake for nearly twenty years—it's generously spiced, and flecked here and there with strands of crushed pineapple and bits of chopped walnuts. The Cream Cheese Frosting is a creamy, slightly tangy contrast to the cake. Note that the frosting should chill for 1 to 2 hours before it is applied to the top of the cake, so plan accordingly.

2 cups unsifted *all-purpose flour*
2 teaspoons baking soda
1½ teaspoons baking powder
½ teaspoon salt
2 teaspoons ground cinnamon
½ teaspoon freshly grated nutmeg
½ teaspoon ground ginger
¼ teaspoon ground allspice
¼ teaspoon ground cloves
1½ cups vegetable oil (such as soybean or canola)
4 extra-large eggs
1¾ cups granulated sugar
¼ cup (firmly packed) dark brown sugar
2 teaspoons vanilla extract
2½ cups grated carrots (about 5 to 6) (use the large holes of a 4-sided boxed hand grater, or a food processor fitted with the medium shredding disk)
One 8-ounce can crushed pineapple in natural juices, well drained
¾ cup chopped walnuts

TO FINISH THE CAKE:
Cream Cheese Frosting (page 105)
or
Brown Sugar Butter Frosting (page 102)

Preheat the oven to 350 degrees. Lightly smear solid shortening inside a 13 by 9 by 2-inch baking pan and dust with all-purpose flour.

Sift together the all-purpose flour, baking soda, baking powder, salt, cinnamon, nutmeg, ginger, allspice, and cloves.

Beat the oil and eggs in the large bowl of an electric mixer on moderate speed for 3 minutes. Add the granulated sugar and dark brown sugar, and beat for 3 minutes longer. Blend in the vanilla extract. Scrape down the sides of the mixing bowl frequently with a rubber spatula to keep the batter even-textured.

On low speed, add the sifted mixture and beat just until the particles of flour are absorbed. Beat in the carrots and crushed pineapple. The batter will be moderately thin. Stir in the walnuts.

Pour and scrape the batter into the pan.

Bake the cake for 55 minutes, or until a wooden pick inserted into the center of the cake is withdrawn without any wet, clinging particles. The baked cake will pull away slightly from the sides of the pan.

Cool the cake in the pan on a rack. Cover the top of the cooled cake with the frosting. For serving, cut the cake into squares.

VARIATION

For *Spiced Carrot Cake with Coconut*, stir ¾ cup sweetened flaked coconut into the cake batter with the walnuts.

Hurry-Up Chocolate Cake

One 13 by 9 by 2-inch cake, serving 16 to 20

Here is a recipe for anyone who needs to create a cake in the shortest time possible, almost without thinking. What to do? Reach for a cake mix and add a handful of other ingredients to reinforce it. This cake is reliable and tasty.

1 box (18.25 ounces) devil's food cake mix, without pudding in the mix
1 box (3.9 ounces) instant chocolate pudding
1¾ cups semisweet chocolate chips
½ cup plain vegetable oil (I use Crisco oil)
¼ cup milk
1¼ cups sour cream
4 extra-large eggs
2 teaspoons vanilla extract

TO FINISH THE CAKE:
Confectioners' sugar (for sprinkling), or
Wellesley Fudge Frosting (page 93), or
Full of Chocolate Frosting (page 95), or
Alice's Chocolate Fudge Frosting (page 96), or
My Mother's Thin and Rich Chocolate Icing (page 94), or
Soft Chocolate Frosting (page 97), or
Creamy Coffee Frosting (page 106)

Preheat the oven to 350 degrees. Lightly smear solid shortening inside a 13 by 9 by 2-inch baking pan and dust with all-purpose flour.

In the large bowl of an electric mixer, combine the cake mix and powdered chocolate pudding mix. Toss the chocolate chips with 1 tablespoon of this dry mixture. Add the oil, milk, sour cream, eggs, and vanilla extract. Beat for 2 minutes on low speed to combine the mixture. Scrape down the sides of the mixing bowl frequently with a rubber spatula to keep the batter even-textured. Beat the batter on moderately high speed for 3 minutes, or until glossy and very smooth. The batter will be somewhat thick. Stir in the chocolate chips, making sure that any of the lingering powdery mix is well incorporated into the batter.

Spoon the batter into the pan.

Bake the cake for 35 to 38 minutes, or until a wooden pick inserted into the center of the cake is withdrawn with some soft, slightly damp and moist crumbs, which is correct. Avoid overbaking the cake.

Cool the cake in the pan on a rack. Simply sift confectioners' sugar lavishly over the top of the cooled cake, or cover the top of the cake with your choice of frosting. For serving, cut the cake into squares.

Oatmeal Cake

One 13 by 9 by 2-inch cake, serving 16 to 20

This excellent oatmeal sheet cake is typical of the cakes that have characterized the best of good-and-simple American baking. At home, my mother and I used the following recipe, which includes some spices, a mixture of solid shortening and butter, and oats softened in boiling water. We usually topped the cake with Coconut-Pecan Frosting.

1 cup "quick-cooking" (not instant) rolled oats
1¼ cups boiling water
1½ cups unsifted *all-purpose flour*
¾ teaspoon baking soda
¼ teaspoon baking powder
¼ teaspoon salt
¾ teaspoon ground cinnamon
½ teaspoon freshly grated nutmeg
¼ teaspoon ground allspice
2 tablespoons unsalted butter, softened
6 tablespoons solid shortening
1 cup granulated sugar
1 cup (firmly packed) light brown sugar
2 extra-large eggs
2 teaspoons vanilla extract

TO FINISH THE CAKE:
Coconut-Pecan Frosting (page 100)

Combine the oats and boiling water in a medium-size heatproof bowl. Stir several times and set aside.

Preheat the oven to 350 degrees. Lightly smear solid shortening inside a 13 by 9 by 2-inch baking pan and dust with all-purpose flour.

Sift the all-purpose flour, baking soda, baking powder, salt, cinnamon, nutmeg, and allspice.

Cream the butter and shortening in the large bowl of an electric mixer on moderate speed for 3 minutes. Add the granulated sugar and beat for 2 minutes on moderately high speed; add the light brown sugar and continue beating for 2 minutes longer. Blend in the eggs, one at a time, beating well after each addition. Blend in the vanilla extract and the oatmeal mixture. Scrape down the sides of the mixing bowl frequently with a rubber spatula to keep the batter even-textured.

On low speed, add the sifted mixture in two additions, beating just until the particles of flour are absorbed. The batter will be medium to medium-thin and pourable.

Pour and scrape the batter into the pan.

Bake the cake for 40 to 45 minutes, or until a wooden pick inserted into the center of the cake is withdrawn without any wet, clinging particles. The baked cake will pull away slightly from the sides of the pan.

Cool the cake in the pan on a rack. Cover the top of the cooled cake with the frosting. For serving, cut the cake into squares.

Apple Cake with Walnuts and Raisins

One 13 by 9 by 2-inch cake, serving 16 to 20

Moist, loaded with shredded apples, and laced with an autumnal cluster of spices—cinnamon, allspice, nutmeg, ginger, and cardamom—this cake is a good keeper, and divine with just-brewed tea or coffee. It's a terrific cake to take to the office for the coffee break, or to a school bake sale.

2½ cups unsifted *all-purpose flour*
2 teaspoons baking powder
½ teaspoon baking soda
½ teaspoon salt
2 teaspoons ground cinnamon
¾ teaspoon freshly grated nutmeg
½ teaspoon ground ginger
¼ teaspoon ground allspice
¼ teaspoon ground cardamom
¾ cup dark raisins
4 extra-large eggs
1¾ cups granulated sugar
¼ cup (firmly packed) light brown sugar
1½ cups plain vegetable oil (I use Crisco oil)
2 teaspoons vanilla extract
3 cups peeled, cored, and shredded apples, such as Stayman, York, Winesap, Rome Beauty, or Empire (see Ingredient Note below)
1 cup chopped walnuts

TO FINISH THE CAKE:
Confectioners' sugar (for sprinkling), or
Vanilla Butter Frosting (page 101), or
Brown Sugar Butter Frosting (page 102), or
Cream Cheese Frosting (page 105)

Preheat the oven to 350 degrees. Lightly smear solid shortening inside a 13 by 9 by 2-inch baking pan and dust with all-purpose flour.

Sift the all-purpose flour, baking powder, baking soda, salt, cinnamon, nutmeg, ginger, allspice, and cardamom. Toss the raisins with 1 tablespoon of the flour mixture.

Beat the eggs in the large bowl of an electric mixer on moderate speed for 2 minutes. Add the granulated sugar and beat on moderately high speed for 2 minutes; add the brown sugar and beat for 1 minute longer. Add the vegetable oil in a steady stream, beating well. Beat in the vanilla extract. The mixture will be relatively thin and shiny. Scrape down the sides of the mixing bowl frequently with a rubber spatula to keep the batter even-textured.

On low speed, alternately add the sifted mixture in two additions, mixing just until the particles of flour have been absorbed. The batter will be moderately thick. Stir in the apples, walnuts, and raisins.

Pour and scrape the batter into the pan.

Bake the cake for 50 minutes, or until a wooden pick inserted into the center of the cake is withdrawn without any wet, clinging particles. The baked cake will pull away slightly from the sides of the pan.

Cool the cake in the pan on a rack. Simply sift confectioners' sugar over the top of the cooled cake, or cover the top of the cake with frosting. For serving, cut the cake into squares.

INGREDIENT NOTE: Three large cooking apples will yield about 3 cups peeled, cored, and shredded apples.

Mint Chocolate Chip Cake

One 13 by 9 by 2-inch cake, serving 16 to 20

Infused with two kinds of chocolate (melted unsweetened chocolate and mint-flavored chocolate chips) and finished with any one of four suave chocolate frostings, this cake is a delicious *and* completely portable treat—take it to a collaborative supper or picnic. It will disappear quickly.

1¼ cups unsifted *cake flour*
1 cup unsifted *all-purpose flour*
1 teaspoon baking soda
½ teaspoon salt
1 cup mint-flavored chocolate chips
10 tablespoons (1 stick plus *2 tablespoons) unsalted butter, softened*
3 tablespoons solid shortening
1¾ cups superfine sugar
3 extra-large eggs
2 teaspoons vanilla extract
3 squares (3 ounces) unsweetened chocolate, melted and cooled
1 cup plus *3½ tablespoons milk* blended with *1 tablespoon distilled white vinegar*

TO FINISH THE CAKE:
Wellesley Fudge Frosting (page 93), or
Full of Chocolate Frosting (page 95), or
Butter and Cream Chocolate Frosting (page 99), or
Soft Chocolate Frosting (page 97)

Preheat the oven to 350 degrees. Lightly smear solid shortening inside a 13 by 9 by 2-inch baking pan and dust with all-purpose flour.

Sift the all-purpose flour and cake flour with the baking soda and salt.

Toss the mint-flavored chips with 1 tablespoon of the sifted mixture.

Cream the butter and shortening in the large bowl of an electric mixer on moderate speed for 4 minutes. Add the superfine sugar in three additions, beating well after each portion is added. Beat on moderately high speed for 3 to 4 minutes. Blend in the eggs, one at a time, beating well after each addition. Blend in the vanilla extract and melted chocolate. Scrape down the sides of the mixing bowl frequently with a rubber spatula to keep the batter even-textured.

On low speed, alternately add the sifted mixture in three additions with the milk-vinegar blend in two additions, beginning and ending with the sifted mixture. The batter will be fluffy-creamy and light. Stir in the mint-flavored chips.

Spoon the batter into the pan.

Bake the cake for 40 minutes, or until a wooden pick inserted into the center of the cake is withdrawn without any clinging particles. The baked cake will pull away slightly from the sides of the pan.

Cool the cake in the pan on a rack. Cover the top of the cooled cake with the frosting. For serving, cut the cake into squares.

Quick Packed-with-Almost-Everything Yellow Cake

One 13 by 9 by 2-inch cake, serving 16 to 20

Miniature chocolate chips, flaked coconut, and chopped walnuts add texture and flavor to this moist sheet cake, made swiftly from a cake mix. For a change, pecans or macadamia nuts can replace the walnuts, and 1½ cups of chopped chocolate-covered almond toffee candy bits can be substituted for the miniature chocolate chips, if you like.

1 box (18.25 ounces) deluxe yellow cake mix (without pudding in the mix)
1 box (3.4 ounces) French vanilla instant pudding
4 extra-large eggs
¾ cup sour cream
¼ cup milk
1 stick (8 tablespoons) unsalted butter, melted and cooled
2 teaspoons vanilla extract
One 12-ounce package miniature semisweet chocolate chips
1 cup sweetened flaked coconut
¾ cup chopped walnuts

TO FINISH THE CAKE:
Confectioners' sugar (for sprinkling), or
Wellesley Fudge Frosting (page 93), or
Full of Chocolate Frosting (page 95), or
Soft Chocolate Frosting (page 97), or
Butter and Cream Chocolate Frosting (page 99)

Preheat the oven to 350 degrees. Lightly smear solid shortening inside a 13 by 9 by 2-inch baking pan and dust with all-purpose flour.

In the large bowl of an electric mixer, combine the cake mix and powdered vanilla pudding mix. Add the eggs, sour cream, milk, melted butter, and vanilla extract. Beat for 2 minutes on low speed to combine the mixture. Scrape down the sides of the mixing bowl frequently with a rubber spatula to keep the batter even-textured. Beat the batter on moderately high speed for 3 minutes, or until very smooth. The batter will be slightly dense, but lustrous. Stir in the chocolate chips, coconut, and walnuts.

Spoon the batter into the pan.

Bake the cake for 40 to 45 minutes, or until a wooden pick inserted into the center of the cake is withdrawn without any wet, clinging particles of batter. The baked cake will pull away slightly from the sides of the pan.

Cool the cake in the pan on a rack. Simply sift confectioners' sugar lavishly over the top of the cooled cake, or cover the top of the cake with your choice of chocolate frosting. For serving, cut the cake into squares.

Soft Spice Cake

One 13 by 9 by 2-inch cake, serving 16 to 20

Squares of this light sheet cake, with its velvety texture and spicy aroma, are particularly welcome in the autumn and winter, and are delicious served with poached pears or apricots, a baked fruit compote (simmer dried fruit in apple cider with a cinnamon stick and split vanilla bean), or applesauce. If the cake has a fruit accompaniment, you might consider omitting the frosting and topping the cake instead with a liberal sifting of confectioners' sugar.

3 cups sifted *cake flour*
3½ teaspoons baking powder
½ teaspoon salt
2½ teaspoons ground cinnamon
1 teaspoon freshly grated nutmeg
1 teaspoon ground ginger
¼ teaspoon ground cloves
¼ teaspoon ground cardamom
10 tablespoons (1 stick plus *2 tablespoons) unsalted butter, softened*
6 tablespoons solid shortening
2 cups superfine sugar
2½ teaspoons vanilla extract
1 cup plus *1 tablespoon milk* blended with *¼ cup light cream*
5 extra-large egg whites
¼ teaspoon cream of tartar

TO FINISH THE CAKE:
Fluffy White Frosting (page 104), or *Vanilla Butter Frosting (page 101)*, or *Brown Sugar Butter Frosting (page 102)*

Preheat the oven to 350 degrees. Lightly smear solid shortening inside a 13 by 9 by 2-inch baking pan and dust with all-purpose flour.

Resift the cake flour with the baking powder, salt, cinnamon, nutmeg, ginger, cloves, and cardamom.

Cream the butter and shortening in the large bowl of an electric mixer on moderate speed for 5 minutes. Add the superfine sugar in four additions, beating well after each portion is added. Beat on moderately high speed for 2 to 3 minutes. Blend in the vanilla extract. Scrape down the sides of the mixing bowl frequently with a rubber spatula to keep the batter even-textured.

On low speed, alternately add the sifted mixture in three additions with the milk-cream blend in two additions, beginning and ending with the sifted mixture.

In a clean, dry bowl, beat the egg whites until frothy, add the cream of tartar, and continue beating until soft, firm peaks are formed. At the softly firm stage, the whites will form a floppy peak when the beaters are lifted up.

Stir about one fourth of the whites into the batter to lighten it. Using a large rubber spatula, lightly but quickly, fold through the remaining whites until well combined.

Spoon the batter into the pan.

Bake the cake for 40 minutes, or until a wooden pick inserted into the center of the cake is withdrawn without any wet, clinging particles. The baked cake will pull away slightly from the sides of the pan.

Cool the cake in the pan on a rack. Cover the top of the cooled cake with the frosting. For serving, cut the cake into squares.

VARIATION

For *Soft Spice Cake with Chocolate Chips*, toss 1¼ cups miniature semisweet chocolate chips with 1 tablespoon of the sifted mixture. Stir the chips into the cake batter *before* incorporating the egg whites. Finish the cake with the Wellesley Fudge Frosting (page 93), *or* Full of Chocolate Frosting (page 95), *or* Soft Chocolate Frosting (page 97).

Blueberry and Spice Cake

One 9 by 9 by 2-inch cake, serving 8

When blueberries are in season, it's worth buying a few extra pints of the fruit to store in the freezer and have at hand for folding into this light-textured cake batter. Serve it warm at breakfast or brunch, or with a fresh blueberry compote for a summery dessert.

1½ cups unsifted *all-purpose flour*
1½ teaspoons baking powder
½ teaspoon baking soda
¼ teaspoon salt
1 teaspoon ground cinnamon
¼ teaspoon ground ginger
¼ teaspoon freshly grated nutmeg
1 cup blueberries, picked over
6 tablespoons (¾ stick) unsalted butter, softened
2 tablespoons solid shortening
½ cup granulated sugar
¼ cup (firmly packed) light brown sugar
2 extra-large eggs
2 teaspoons vanilla extract
1 cup sour cream
½ cup chopped walnuts

FOR THE CINNAMON-BUTTER CRUMB TOPPING:
¼ cup granulated sugar
¼ cup light brown sugar
1 tablespoon ground cinnamon
1 tablespoon all-purpose flour
3 tablespoons unsalted butter, cold, cut into small cubes

Preheat the oven to 350 degrees. Lightly smear solid shortening inside a 9 by 9 by 2-inch baking pan and dust with all-purpose flour.

Sift the all-purpose flour, baking powder, baking soda, salt, cinnamon, ginger, and nutmeg. Toss the blueberries with 2 teaspoons of the sifted mixture.

Cream the butter and shortening in the large bowl of an electric mixer on moderate speed for 3 to 4 minutes. Add the granulated sugar and light brown sugar; beat on moderate speed for 4 to 5 minutes. Blend in the eggs, one at a time, beating well after each addition. Blend in the vanilla extract. Scrape down the sides of the mixing bowl frequently with a rubber spatula to keep the batter even-textured.

On low speed, beat in half of the sifted mixture, the sour cream, then the balance of the sifted mixture. Stir in the blueberries and walnuts.

Spoon the batter into the pan.

In a small bowl, thoroughly combine the granulated sugar, light brown sugar, cinnamon, and flour. Scatter over the butter and crumble the mixture between your fingertips to form a coarse, slightly lumpy topping. Sprinkle the mixture evenly over the top of the batter.

Bake the cake for 35 to 40 minutes, or until a wooden pick inserted into the center of the cake is withdrawn without any wet, clinging particles. The baked cake will pull away slightly from the sides of the pan.

Cool the cake in the pan on a rack. For serving, cut the cake into squares.

NOTE: To freeze the fresh blueberries of summer for fall and winter baking, pick over for stems and leaves, then rinse quickly in cool water and dry thoroughly on sheets of paper toweling. Scatter the berries on a rimmed baking sheet in a single layer and freeze. When the berries are frozen and as firm as marbles, pack them up in individual freezer-safe bags. It's wise to place about 1 cup of berries in each bag. Seal the bags well and identify the contents on a strip of freezer tape.

White Coconut and Macadamia Nut Cake

One 13 by 9 by 2-inch cake, serving 16 to 20

I consider this cake one of my prize heirloom recipes. It is light and soft, and blanketed with a generous amount of billowy frosting and flaked coconut. This is a cake that never disappoints.

3 cups sifted cake flour
2½ teaspoons baking powder
½ teaspoon salt
8 tablespoons (1 stick) unsalted butter, softened
½ cup (8 tablespoons) solid shortening
1¾ cups superfine sugar
2½ teaspoons vanilla extract
½ teaspoon almond extract
1¼ cups milk
¾ cup chopped macadamia nuts
½ cup sweetened flaked coconut
4 extra-large egg whites
¼ teaspoon cream of tartar

TO FINISH THE CAKE:
Fluffy White Frosting (page 104) or *Vanilla Butter Frosting (page 101)*
About 2½ to 3 cups sweetened flaked coconut

Preheat the oven to 350 degrees. Lightly smear solid shortening inside a 13 by 9 by 2-inch baking pan and dust with all-purpose flour.

Resift the cake flour with the baking powder and salt.

Cream the butter and shortening in the large bowl of an electric mixer on moderate speed for 5 minutes. Add the superfine sugar in three additions, beating well after each portion is added. Beat on moderately high speed for 3 minutes. Blend in the vanilla extract and almond extract. Scrape down the sides of the mixing bowl frequently with a rubber spatula to keep the batter even-textured.

On low speed, alternately add the sifted mixture in three additions with the milk in two additions, beginning and ending with the sifted mixture. At this point, the batter will be moderately thick and creamy, and will lighten up when the egg whites are added. Stir in the macadamia nuts and the coconut.

In a clean, dry mixing bowl, beat the egg whites until frothy, add the cream of tartar, and continue beating until moderately firm peaks are formed. The whites will hold a straight peak when the beaters are lifted up, but will look moist and shiny, and not at all dry.

Rapidly stir about one-fourth of the whites into the batter to lighten it. Using a large rubber spatula, lightly but quickly, fold through the remaining whites until well combined.

Spoon the batter into the pan.

Bake the cake for 37 to 40 minutes, or until a wooden pick inserted into the center of the cake is withdrawn without any wet, clinging particles. The baked cake will pull away slightly from the sides of the pan.

Cool the cake in the pan on a rack. Cover the top of the cooled cake with the frosting, then generously sprinkle over the flaked coconut. For serving, cut the cake into squares.

Spiced Pumpkin Cake

One 13 by 9 by 2-inch cake, serving 16 to 20

A choice pumpkin-tinged cake, perfect for cool weather picnics or a celebrate-the-harvest weekend dinner, is moist, tinged with five spices, and tenderized with a little buttermilk. The version that replaces the raisins and walnuts with miniature semisweet chocolate chips (see Variation) is, of course, for those who require a little chocolate with their pumpkin.

3 cups unsifted *all-purpose flour*
1½ teaspoons baking powder
¾ teaspoon baking soda
½ teaspoon salt
2½ teaspoons ground cinnamon
1 teaspoon freshly grated nutmeg
½ teaspoon ground allspice
½ teaspoon ground ginger
¼ teaspoon ground cloves
½ cup dark raisins
12 tablespoons (1½ sticks) unsalted butter, softened
4 tablespoons solid shortening
2¾ cups superfine sugar
4 extra-large eggs
2 extra-large egg yolks
One *16-ounce can (2 cups) "solid pack" pumpkin puree (not pumpkin pie filling)*
¼ cup buttermilk blended with *1 tablespoon vanilla extract*
¾ cup chopped walnuts

TO FINISH THE CAKE:
Confectioners' sugar (for sprinkling), or
Vanilla Butter Frosting (page 101), or
Brown Sugar Butter Frosting (page 102)

Preheat the oven to 350 degrees. Lightly smear solid shortening inside a 13 by 9 by 2-inch baking pan and dust with all-purpose flour.

Sift the all-purpose flour with the baking powder, baking soda, salt, cinnamon, nutmeg, allspice, ginger, and cloves. Toss the raisins with 1 teaspoon of the sifted mixture.

Cream the butter and shortening in the large bowl of an electric mixer on moderate speed for 4 minutes. Add the superfine sugar in three additions, beating well after each portion is added. Beat on moderately high speed for 3 to 4 minutes. Blend in the whole eggs, one at a time, beating well after each addition. Blend in the egg yolks. Beat in the pumpkin puree and buttermilk-vanilla blend. The mixture will look curdled, which is correct for this stage of the mixing. Scrape down the sides of the mixing bowl frequently with a rubber spatula to keep the batter even-textured.

On low speed, add the sifted mixture in three additions, beating just until the flour is absorbed. The batter will look very fluffy, almost like an ultra-smooth, well-beaten buttercream frosting. Stir in the raisins and walnuts.

Spoon the batter into the pan.

Bake the cake for about 50 minutes, or until a wooden pick inserted into the center of the cake is withdrawn without any wet, clinging particles. The baked cake will pull away slightly from the sides of the pan.

Cool the cake in the pan on a rack. Sprinkle confectioners' sugar generously on top of the cake, or cover the top with the frosting. For serving, cut the cake into squares.

VARIATION

For *Spiced Pumpkin Cake with Miniature Chocolate Chips*, omit the raisins and walnuts. *Decrease* the cinnamon to 1 teaspoon, the nutmeg to ½ teaspoon, and the allspice and ginger to ¼ teaspoon. Toss one 12-ounce bag of miniature semisweet chocolate chips with 1 tablespoon of the sifted mixture and add them after the flour has been blended into the batter. Frost with Wellesley Fudge Frosting (page 93), *or* Full of Chocolate Frosting (page 95), *or* Soft Chocolate Frosting (page 97), *or* Sour Cream Chocolate Frosting 209½ (page 98).

Rich Mocha Cake

One 13 by 9 by 2-inch cake, serving 16 to 20

Very strong black coffee (preferably an espresso roast) gives this chocolate cake its soft mocha essence. The basis for this recipe is an egg-enriched butter cake formula, one which has been worked out to incorporate chocolate, coffee, and sour cream. This light-textured sheet cake is splendid when paired with an indulgent frosting, such as Alice's Chocolate Fudge Frosting or Wellesley Fudge Frosting.

1½ cups unsifted *all-purpose flour*
1½ cups unsifted *cake flour*
¾ teaspoon baking soda
¼ teaspoon baking powder
½ teaspoon salt
10 tablespoons (1 stick plus *2 tablespoons) unsalted butter, softened*
2 tablespoons solid shortening
2 cups superfine sugar
4 extra-large eggs
2 extra-large egg yolks
1 tablespoon vanilla extract
4 squares (4 ounces) unsweetened chocolate, melted and cooled
¾ cup sour cream blended with *¼ cup cool, strong black coffee*

TO FINISH THE CAKE:

Wellesley Fudge Frosting (page 93), or
Alice's Chocolate Fudge Frosting (page 96), or
Full of Chocolate Frosting (page 95), or
Soft Chocolate Frosting (page 97), or
Butter and Cream Chocolate Frosting (page 99), or
Sour Cream Chocolate Frosting 209½ (page 98), or
Creamy Coffee Frosting (page 106)

Preheat the oven to 350 degrees. Lightly smear solid shortening inside a 13 by 9 by 2-inch baking pan and dust with all-purpose flour.

Sift the all-purpose flour, cake flour, baking soda, baking powder, and salt.

Cream the butter and shortening in the large bowl of an electric mixer on moderate speed for 4 to 5 minutes. Add the superfine sugar in three additions, beating well after each portion is added. Beat on moderately high speed for 2 minutes. Blend in the whole eggs, one at a time, beating well after each addition, then blend in the egg yolks. Blend in the vanilla extract and melted chocolate. Scrape down the sides of the mixing bowl frequently with a rubber spatula to keep the batter even-textured.

On low speed, alternately add the sifted mixture in three additions with the sour cream–coffee mixture in two additions, beginning and ending with the sifted mixture.

Pour and scrape the batter into the pan.

Bake the cake for 35 to 40 minutes, or until a wooden pick inserted into the center of the cake is withdrawn without any wet, clinging particles. The baked cake will pull away slightly from the sides of the pan.

Cool the cake in the pan on a rack. Cover the top of the cooled cake with the frosting. For serving, cut the cake into squares.

VARIATIONS

For *Rich Mocha Cake with Miniature Chocolate Chips*, toss ¾ cup miniature semisweet chocolate chips with 2 teaspoons of the sifted mixture. Stir the chips into the batter just before spooning it into the pan.

For *Rich Mocha Cake with Walnuts*, toss ¾ cup chopped walnuts with 1 teaspoon of the sifted mixture and stir into the batter just before spooning it into the pan.

Lemon Cake

One 13 by 9 by 2-inch cake, serving 16 to 20

The soft lemon flavor of this cake is sharpened with a tangy lemon icing. In the summertime, serve squares of cake with a berry "salad" that combines raspberries, blueberries, and blackberries with strawberries along with splashes of orange juice to moisten the fruit.

2 cups sifted all-purpose flour
1 cup sifted cake flour
2½ teaspoons baking powder
½ teaspoon salt
12 tablespoons (1½ sticks) unsalted butter, softened
4 tablespoons solid shortening
2 cups superfine sugar
4 extra-large eggs
2 teaspoons finely grated lemon zest
2 teaspoons lemon extract
1 cup milk

TO FINISH THE CAKE:
Lemon Icing (page 103) or
Fluffy White Frosting (page 104)

Preheat the oven to 375 degrees. Lightly smear solid shortening inside a 13 by 9 by 2-inch baking pan and dust with all-purpose flour.

Resift the all-purpose flour and cake flour with the baking powder and salt twice.

Cream the butter and shortening in the large bowl of an electric mixer on moderate speed for 4 minutes. Add the superfine sugar in three additions, beating well after each portion is added. Beat on moderately high speed for 4 minutes. Blend in the eggs, one at a time, beating well after each addition. Blend in the lemon zest and lemon extract. Scrape down the sides of the mixing bowl frequently with a rubber spatula to keep the batter even-textured.

On low speed, alternately add the sifted mixture in three additions with the milk in two additions, beginning and ending with the sifted mixture.

Pour and scrape the batter into the pan.

Bake the cake for 30 to 35 minutes, or until a wooden pick inserted into the center of the cake is withdrawn without any wet, clinging particles. The baked cake will pull away slightly from the sides of the pan and the top will be a light brown color.

Cool the cake in the pan on a rack. Cover the top of the cooled cake with the icing or frosting. For serving, cut the cake into squares.

VARIATIONS

For *Lemon–Poppy Seed Cake*, blend ¼ cup poppy seeds into the batter just before spooning it into the cake pan.

For *Lemon-Walnut Cake*, toss ¾ cup chopped walnuts with 1 teaspoon of the sifted mixture and stir into the batter just before spooning it into the cake pan.

Birthday White Cake

One 13 by 9 by 2-inch cake, serving 16 to 20

Aside from candles and scoops of ice cream, it's really nostalgia and sentiment that accompanies a birthday cake. For some, a cake that is utterly chocolate is a must; for others, a white cake topped with chocolate or vanilla frosting. The light, almost fluffy quality of this cake is what appeals to me and its texture is an excellent complement to any of the rich, creamy frostings in this book. This is a cake that I've been baking for many years.

2 cups unsifted *all-purpose flour*
1 cup unsifted *cake flour*
2½ teaspoons baking powder
½ teaspoon salt
½ teaspoon freshly grated nutmeg
10 tablespoons (1 stick plus *2 tablespoons) solid shortening*
6 tablespoons (¾ stick) unsalted butter, softened
2 cups superfine sugar
2½ teaspoons vanilla extract
1¼ cups milk
5 extra-large egg whites
⅛ teaspoon cream of tartar

TO FINISH THE CAKE:
Wellesley Fudge Frosting (page 93), or
Full of Chocolate Frosting (page 95), or
Soft Chocolate Frosting (page 97), or
Butter and Cream Chocolate Frosting (page 99), or
Vanilla Butter Frosting (page 101), or
Sour Cream Chocolate Frosting 209½(page 98), or
Lemon Icing (page 103)

Preheat the oven to 375 degrees. Lightly smear solid shortening inside a 13 by 9 by 2-inch baking pan and dust with all-purpose flour.

Sift the all-purpose flour and cake flour with the baking powder, salt, and nutmeg.

Cream the shortening and butter in the large bowl of an electric mixer on moderate speed for 3 to 4 minutes. Add 1½ cups of the superfine sugar in three additions, beating well after each portion is added. Blend in the vanilla extract. Scrape down the sides of the mixing bowl frequently with a rubber spatula to keep the batter even-textured.

On low speed, alternately add the sifted mixture in three additions with the milk in two additions, beginning and ending with the sifted mixture.

Using a handheld electric mixer, beat the egg whites in a clean, dry, deep bowl until foamy, add the cream of tartar, and continue beating until very soft, floppy peaks are formed. Add the remaining ½ cup superfine sugar and continue beating until firm (not stiff) peaks are formed. Stir about one-quarter of the beaten whites into the batter, then fold through the remaining whites quickly but thoroughly, breaking up any large patches. Small flecks can remain in the batter.

Spoon the batter into the pan.

Bake the cake for about 40 minutes, or until a wooden pick inserted into the center of the cake is withdrawn without any wet, clinging particles. The baked cake will pull away slightly from the sides of the pan.

Cool the cake in the pan on a rack. Cover the top of the cooled cake with the frosting. For serving, cut the cake into squares.

VARIATIONS

For *Birthday White Cake with Coconut*, blend 1 cup sweetened flaked coconut into the batter after the sifted flour mixture and the milk have been added, but before the egg whites are folded through. Finish the cake with Fluffy White Frosting (page 104) *or* Vanilla Butter Frosting (page 101).

For *Birthday White Cake with Miniature Semisweet Chocolate Chips*, omit the nutmeg. Toss 1 cup miniature semisweet chocolate chips with 1 tablespoon of the sifted mixture. Blend the chips into the batter after the sifted flour mixture and the milk have been added, but before the eggs whites are folded through. Finish the cake with Wellesley Fudge Frosting (page 93), *or* Full of Chocolate Frosting (page 95), *or* Soft Chocolate Frosting (page 97), *or* Sour Cream Chocolate Frosting 209½ (page 98), *or* Vanilla Butter Frosting (page 101).

7

Frostings and Icings

American frostings and icings are sturdy, sweet concoctions mixed in quantities generous enough to peak, swirl, and smooth around and about a layer or sheet cake. A typical vanilla or chocolate frosting gets its bulk from confectioners' sugar beaten with butter, flavoring, and enough liquid to make it soft and spreadable. Such a frosting, whose primary ingredient is confectioners' sugar, is usually made in a free-standing electric mixer or in a mixing bowl with a sturdy handheld mixer, away from any heat source (although any chocolate is melted and the butter is either softened or melted first). It's lush, easy to apply to baked cake layers, and enormously appealing for its traditional flavor.

Sometimes, a confectioners' sugar frosting can taste chalky or "starchy." Some years ago, by accident, I came upon an interesting technique for mellowing this occasional chalkiness. After the frosting is beaten to a light and creamy stage, having added all of the confectioners' sugar, place it in a large heatproof bowl and set it over another bowl containing about 1 to 2 inches of very hot water. (The water should not be deep enough to touch the bottom of the bowl containing the frosting.) Stir the frosting for 2 to 3 minutes; this will "cure" the mixture and ripen the flavor. Take care to keep the frosting in motion to prevent it from melting down. The frostings in this book that will benefit from this added procedure are: Wellesley Fudge Frosting (page 93), Full of Chocolate Frosting (page 95), Soft Chocolate Frosting (page 97), Butter and Cream Chocolate Frosting (page 99), Vanilla Butter Frosting (page 101), and Creamy Coffee Frosting (page 106).

Another type of frosting, generically termed "seven minute," is made with egg whites, granulated sugar, and water (plus, on occasion, a small amount of corn syrup, cream of tartar, and vanilla extract), beaten to a thick fluffiness in a double boiler directly over low heat; the phrase "seven minute" refers to the amount of time it takes to concoct a frosting that is thick enough to hold its shape. You can sweep and peak a seven-minute frosting over a cake quickly, and with exceptional ease.

An icing, as opposed to a frosting, is also spread over a sheet cake, or on top and between cake layers, but it is much thinner than a frosting. Most icings are pourable and, for that reason, are easiest to use on a cake if they are first spooned into a large measuring cup, and carefully poured onto the cake. As soon as enough icing flows onto the cake, it can be leveled and smoothed over with a flexible palette knife.

Wellesley Fudge Frosting

Makes about 3½ to 4 cups

Thick, indulgent, and quite simple to make, this is the classic frosting made with Baker's unsweetened chocolate and paired with layers of the Wellesley Fudge Cake on page 46 (and sometimes published with that recipe). It was passed down to me from "Baker's Chocolate and Coconut Favorites," a pamphlet produced by the General Foods Corporation years ago; the name of the frosting surfaces as "Easy Chocolate Frosting," although my mother and I always referred to it as "that fudgy Wellesley chocolate frosting." Occasionally, we found that superb frosting needs a little extra milk. It's also a perfect match to nearly any of the yellow, white, or chocolate layer cakes in this book.

4 squares (4 ounces) unsweetened chocolate
4 tablespoons unsalted butter
4 cups (one 1-pound box) unsifted *confectioners' sugar*
⅛ teaspoon salt
½ cup milk, plus *additional 1 to 2 tablespoons*, *as needed*
1 teaspoon vanilla extract

Melt the chocolate and butter in a small, heavy saucepan over low heat (preferably enameled cast iron). Cool slightly. Pour and scrape the chocolate mixture into a large mixing bowl. Sift the confectioners' sugar with the salt. Beat in about half of the confectioners' sugar, ¼ cup milk, and the vanilla extract. Beat on moderate speed for 3 minutes. Add the remaining confectioners' sugar and ¼ cup milk and continue beating for 3 to 4 minutes longer, or until quite smooth. Add additional milk, 1 tablespoon at a time, if the frosting seems too thick to spread easily. In a cool kitchen, or on a cold day in winter, you may need to add an additional 1 to 2 tablespoons of milk.

Use the frosting immediately on thoroughly cooled layer and sheet cakes.

My Mother's Thin and Rich Chocolate Icing

Makes about 2¾ cups

One of my very favorite cake coverings, this icing is made entirely in a saucepan. Just removed from the heat, it is thin, but it thickens as it cools. It's important to remember that this is a light—but chocolaty—topping and not as billowy as those frostings made with confectioners' sugar.

4½ squares (4½ ounces) unsweetened chocolate, coarsely chopped
9 tablespoons (1 stick plus *1 tablespoon) unsalted butter, cut in chunks*
¾ cup granulated sugar
1 tablespoon plus *1½ teaspoons cornstarch*
½ cup milk
¼ cup light cream
Pinch of salt
1¼ teaspoons vanilla extract

Melt the chocolate and butter in a medium-size, heavy saucepan over low heat. Thoroughly blend together the granulated sugar and cornstarch in a mixing bowl. Blend the milk and cream into the cornstarch mixture. Off the heat, stir the sugar-milk-cream mixture and salt into the chocolate mixture, stirring well. Bring to a boil over moderately high heat, stirring. When the mixture reaches the boil, boil for 1 minute or until thickened. The icing will lightly coat the back of a spoon. Remove from the heat and stir in the vanilla. Let the frosting cool for 5 to 9 minutes, stirring slowly but frequently. Spoon and spread the frosting over and between thoroughly cooled layer and sheet cakes.

NOTE: This recipe appears in slightly different form in *Country Cakes: A Homestyle Treasury* (New York: Harper & Row, 1989), the second cookbook in my country baking trilogy, and republished in *A Country Baking Treasury* (New York: HarperCollins Publishers, 1995).

Full of Chocolate Frosting

Makes about 3½ cups

Over ¼ pound of unsweetened chocolate and ½ cup of heavy cream make this frosting luxurious.

6 tablespoons (¾ stick) unsalted butter, cut into chunks
5 squares (5 ounces) unsweetened chocolate, chopped
Pinch of salt
4 cups (one 1-pound box) confectioners' sugar, sifted
½ cup heavy cream, or more as needed (see Ingredient Note)
2 teaspoons vanilla extract

Place the butter and chocolate in a small, heavy saucepan (preferably enameled cast iron), set over low heat, and melt the chocolate completely. Stir well. Remove from the heat. Let butter-chocolate mixture cool for 5 to 6 minutes, stirring once or twice.

Pour and scrape the butter-chocolate mixture into a large mixing bowl. Using a handheld electric mixer, beat in the salt, about one-third of the confectioners' sugar, and half of the cream. Blend in another third of the sugar, the remaining cream, and the vanilla extract. Beat in the remaining third of sugar. Continue beating for 2 to 3 minutes on moderate speed, or until the frosting is creamy-textured. Add additional cream, 1 teaspoon at a time, if the frosting appears too thick to spread smoothly and easily. The density of the frosting will be about medium-thick.

Use the frosting immediately on thoroughly cooled layer and sheet cakes.

INGREDIENT NOTE: Light cream may be substituted for the heavy cream, but since light cream is less dense, begin with ⅓ cup of cream, then add the remaining cream by tablespoons to achieve a spreadable frosting.

Alice's Chocolate Fudge Frosting

Makes about 3 cups

This frosting is designed to cover the top of Alice's Chocolate Pan Cake on page 60 (and this recipe is also taken from my book *Country Cakes: A Homestyle Treasury* [New York: Harper & Row, 1989], which is now part of a larger book called *A Country Baking Treasury* [New York: HarperCollins Publishers, 1995]). In the recipe I have from my friend Alice Romejko, the amount of milk called for is 6 tablespoons. I use 5 tablespoons of milk and 1 tablespoon of light cream. The frosting is full of chocolate, creamy, sweet, and quite fudgy. It's wise to make the frosting while the cake is baking (cover it with a sheet of plastic wrap when completed), so that the frosting is ready to apply to the top of the cake.

This frosting also makes a terrific topping for the Hurry-Up Chocolate Cake (page 66) or the Rich Mocha Cake (page 84).

8 tablespoons (1 stick) unsalted butter, cut into chunks
2 squares (2 ounces) unsweetened chocolate, chopped
5 tablespoons milk
1 tablespoon light cream
4 cups (one 1-pound box) confectioners' sugar, sifted
1 teaspoon vanilla extract
Pinch of salt
1 cup chopped pecans (see Ingredient Note)

Place the butter, chocolate, milk, and cream in a large saucepan, set over low heat, and cook, stirring occasionally, until the chocolate is completely melted. Remove from the heat, pour and scrape into a mixing bowl, and beat in the sugar 1 cup at a time with the vanilla extract and salt. Stir in the pecans. Immediately spread the frosting over the top of the warm sheet cake.

INGREDIENT NOTE: I often substitute chopped walnuts for the pecans.

METHOD NOTE: Sometimes, instead of blending the pecans into the frosting, I'll vary the look of the cake by sprinkling them on top of the frosted cake.

Soft Chocolate Frosting

Makes about 2¾ cups

Sheet cakes, especially plain vanilla or chocolate, are simply wonderful topped with this creamy frosting. It is, perhaps, one of the more delicate frostings you'll encounter made with confectioners' sugar.

3 squares (3 ounces) unsweetened chocolate, melted and cooled
6 tablespoons (¾ stick) unsalted butter, softened
3 cups unsifted *confectioners' sugar*
Pinch of salt
2 teaspoons vanilla extract
¼ cup light cream
¼ cup sour cream (see Ingredient Note)

Place the melted chocolate, butter, 1 cup confectioners' sugar, salt, and vanilla in a large bowl and, using a handheld electric mixer, beat for 1 minute on moderate speed. Add the light cream and half of the remaining sugar. Beat for 1 minute on high speed. Add the remaining sugar and the sour cream. Beat for 2 minutes on high speed or until well combined and satiny.

Use the frosting immediately on thoroughly cooled layer and sheet cakes.

INGREDIENT NOTE: Heavy cream may be substituted for the sour cream.

Sour Cream Chocolate Frosting 209½

Makes about 3 cups

This recipe comes from Jason Wolin, and was created to accompany his Sour Cream Chocolate Cake 209½ (page 30). The success of this recipe is dependent on beating the ingredients together thoroughly and well, as indicated in the method, to develop its volume, consistency, and luster. For this thorough beating, I use my Kitchen Aid mixer fitted with the wire whisk beater: the depth of the bowl, size of the beater, and power of the mixer all contribute to creating a beautifully light frosting. (Using a handheld electric mixer and a deep bowl will also produce a good frosting, but I would recommend increasing the final 6-minute beating time to 10 minutes.)

One of the joys of this frosting is its silky quality, allowing you to spread it over and over the cake without losing a trace of sheen or substance. And so, if the telephone or doorbell rings and you are called away from icing the cake, never panic, as the frosting stays soft for some time.

5 ounces (5 squares) unsweetened chocolate
8 tablespoons (1 stick) unsalted butter
2¼ cups unsifted *confectioners' sugar*
1 cup sour cream
1 teaspoon vanilla extract

Melt the chocolate and butter in a heavy saucepan over low heat. Remove from the heat and cool to lukewarm.

Place the sugar and sour cream in the large bowl of an electric mixer and beat for 3 minutes on high speed. Add the vanilla extract and melted chocolate-butter mixture. Beat the frosting on high speed for a *full 6 minutes*, when it will turn light, glossy, and shimmery.

Use the frosting on thoroughly cooled layer and sheet cakes.

INGREDIENT NOTE: Although not a part of the recipe as it came to me from Jason Wolin with the Sour Cream Chocolate Cake 209½, a small pinch of salt added with the vanilla and melted chocolate-butter mixture seems to bring out the flavor of the chocolate.

Butter and Cream Chocolate Frosting

Makes 3 cups

Creamy, rich, and smooth, this frosting is ideal to use with yellow, white, chocolate, or banana layer or sheet cakes.

8 tablespoons (1 stick) unsalted butter, softened, melted, and cooled
4 squares (4 ounces) unsweetened chocolate, melted and cooled
1½ teaspoons vanilla extract
Pinch of salt
4½ cups (one 1-pound box plus *½ cup)* unsifted *confectioners' sugar*
½ cup light cream

In a medium-size mixing bowl, blend together the butter, chocolate, vanilla extract, and salt. Add half of the confectioners' sugar and cream and beat, using an electric handheld mixer, on moderate speed for 1 minute. Add the remaining confectioners' sugar and beat for 3 to 4 minutes longer, or until very smooth. The frosting should be medium-thick. If it appears too soft, add more confectioners' sugar, 1 tablespoon at a time. Cover the frosting and chill it for 15 minutes before using.

Coconut-Pecan Frosting

Makes about 2½ cups

This frosting, made with Baker's Angel Flake Coconut, is one of the variations printed along with the recipe for German Sweet Chocolate Cake customarily made with Baker's German's Sweet Chocolate Bar. Some years after my mother and I began to bake the cake, someone sent me a pamphlet produced by the General Foods Corporation titled "Baker's Chocolate and Coconut Favorites" and this frosting appears in it. The version that accompanied my mother's recipe used the same ingredients but more of them (an additional ½ cup *each* of evaporated milk, sugar, and pecans, an extra egg yolk, 4 tablespoons more butter, ⅔ cup more coconut, and ½ teaspoon more vanilla). Both ways, it's opulent and delicious, and a tasteful contrast to the chocolate cake layers.

1 cup evaporated milk
1 cup granulated sugar
3 egg yolks, slightly beaten
8 tablespoons (1 stick) unsalted butter
1 teaspoon vanilla extract
1⅓ cups sweetened flaked coconut
1 cup chopped pecans

Combine the evaporated milk, sugar, egg yolks, butter, and vanilla in a heavy (preferably enameled cast iron) saucepan. Place over moderate heat and cook uncovered, stirring, until thickened. This should take about 12 minutes.

Remove the saucepan from the heat, add the coconut and pecans, and stir until the frosting has cooled slightly, about 5 minutes, or longer if necessary. The frosting should be somewhat shiny, moderately thick but still spoonable. Use the frosting immediately.

INGREDIENT NOTE: Over the years, I've found that using ½ cup granulated sugar and ½ cup (firmly packed) light brown sugar also produces a delicious frosting. And walnuts substitute nicely for the pecans.

Vanilla Butter Frosting

Makes about 2⅔ cups

A basic vanilla frosting made with butter, sugar, milk, and vanilla extract is a good match for white or yellow cakes. Use it, too, for spreading over and about layers of coconut cake, then top it all with plenty of flaked coconut.

6 tablespoons (¾ stick) unsalted butter, softened
3½ cups confectioners' sugar, sifted
3 tablespoons milk
Pinch of salt
2 teaspoons vanilla extract

Place the butter in a large mixing bowl and, using a handheld electric mixer, beat for 30 seconds on moderate speed. Beat in 1 cup of the confectioners' sugar. Add half of the milk, the salt, and half of the remaining sugar. Beat on moderately high speed until the sugar is incorporated, about 1 to 2 minutes. Add the remaining milk and sugar and the vanilla extract, and continue beating until creamy-textured and soft. This will take about 1 to 2 minutes longer. If the frosting is too stiff, beat in extra milk, 1 teaspoon at a time; if it fails to hold its shape softly in a spoon or on a spatula, blend in additional confectioners' sugar 1 tablespoon at a time.

Use the frosting immediately on thoroughly cooled layer and sheet cakes.

Brown Sugar Butter Frosting

Makes 2 cups

The best way to create a light butterscotch-flavored frosting is to simmer brown sugar, butter, and cream in a saucepan until lightly thickened and shiny, and blend that with vanilla extract and confectioners' sugar. The frosting is easy to work with, and especially suits my Spiced Pumpkin Cake (page 82), Spiced Carrot Cake (page 64), Soft Spice Cake (page 76), and the Apple Cake with Walnuts and Raisins (page 70).

6 tablespoons (¾ stick) unsalted butter, cut into chunks
½ cup (firmly packed) dark brown sugar
¼ cup light cream
Pinch of salt
2 teaspoons vanilla extract
3⅓ cups unsifted *confectioners' sugar*

Put the butter, brown sugar, cream, and salt in a small, heavy saucepan (preferably enameled cast iron). Set over low heat and cook until the sugar has dissolved completely. Raise the heat to moderate and simmer the brown sugar mixture for 3 to 4 minutes, or until *slightly* syrupy and only lightly condensed. Remove the saucepan from the heat and stir in the vanilla extract. Cool for 2 minutes.

Place the confectioners' sugar in a large mixing bowl and pour over the brown sugar mixture. Beat the frosting with a handheld electric mixer for 3 minutes, or until light and creamy.

Use the frosting immediately on thoroughly cooled layer and sheet cakes.

Lemon Icing

Makes about 1½ cups

Light and full of the tang of lemon, this icing is easy to spread over sheet cakes, and makes a supremely good sweet-and-tart glaze for gingerbread, spice, honey, or nut cakes. The icing in the quantity you see here amply covers a 13 by 9 by 2-inch sheet cake. For an icing that coats the cake in a thinner layer, use the alternate proportions below (see Note).

4 tablespoons (½ stick) unsalted butter, softened
3 cups unsifted *confectioners' sugar*
1½ teaspoons milk
6 tablespoons freshly squeezed lemon juice
1 teaspoon grated lemon zest

Place the butter in a medium-size bowl and, using a handheld electric mixer, beat for 30 seconds. Sift over the confectioners' sugar. Add the milk and lemon juice. Beat the icing for 1 to 2 minutes on low speed, or until well combined and very smooth, scraping down the sides of the bowl to keep the mixture even-textured. Blend in the lemon zest.

Use the icing immediately on a *slightly* warm or thoroughly cooled sheet cake.

NOTE: For *1 cup of lemon icing*, use 3 tablespoons unsalted butter, 2¼ cups *unsifted* confectioners' sugar, 1 teaspoon milk, 4½ tablespoons lemon juice, and ½ teaspoon grated lemon zest. Follow the directions for preparing the icing as outlined above.

Fluffy White Frosting

Makes about 3¾ cups

The texture of this frosting is marshmallow-like and soft. It's traditionally used to ice a dark devil's food cake, white cake, or coconut cake.

4 teaspoons powdered egg whites (see Ingredient Note)
¼ cup lukewarm water
1⅓ cups plus *2 tablespoons superfine sugar*
⅓ cup cold water
⅛ teaspoon cream of tartar
1½ teaspoons white corn syrup
1 teaspoon vanilla extract

Whisk together the powdered egg whites and lukewarm water in a small bowl, mixing thoroughly to completely dissolve the whites. Place the egg-white solution, superfine sugar, cold water, cream of tartar, and corn syrup in the top of a double boiler. Place over the bottom saucepan of the double boiler, filled with *barely* simmering water (the water should come up ¼ inch *short* of the bottom of the top saucepan, and never touch the pan holding the frosting ingredients), and set over low heat.

Using a handheld electric mixer, beat the frosting mixture on moderate speed for 7 minutes, or until thick, shiny, and voluminous. Beat the frosting continuously and take care that the water remains at a very low bubble, lest the mixture turn granular and curdle. After 7 minutes, carefully remove the top saucepan from the water bath and wipe dry the bottom and sides. Add the vanilla extract and continue beating for 1 minute.

Use the frosting immediately over a cooled layer or sheet cake.

INGREDIENT NOTE: This frosting is made with powdered egg whites. I use Just Whites, a fine product distributed by the Deb-El Foods Corporation, 2 Papetti Plaza, Elizabeth, NJ 07206; it's packaged in an 8-ounce container with a resealable lid. Using powdered egg whites is an easy, accessible way to make a frosting.

For this recipe, and others, I follow the chart on the container, which instructs the cook on how to use the whites by adding a quantity of lukewarm water to each measurement of the powdered whites. For example, to produce the equivalent of 1 white, you combine 2 teaspoons of Just Whites with 2 tablespoons of lukewarm water.

Cream Cheese Frosting

Makes 3 cups

Creamy, light, slightly tangy, and very smooth.

One 8-ounce package cream cheese, softened
4 tablespoons (¼ stick) unsalted butter, softened
2 teaspoons vanilla extract
1 tablespoon milk
2¾ cups unsifted *confectioners' sugar*

Beat the cream cheese and butter in the large bowl of an electric mixer on moderate speed for 3 to 4 minutes. Add the vanilla, milk, and about one-third of the confectioners' sugar. Beat for 1 minute. Add the balance of the confectioners' sugar and beat on moderate speed until light and soft, about 3 minutes longer. Cover and refrigerate for 1 to 2 hours, or until well chilled and dense enough to spread.

Just before using, thoroughly beat the frosting until slightly fluffy and spreadable. Use the frosting on cooled layer and sheet cakes.

Creamy Coffee Frosting

Makes about 3 cups

The soft coffee flavor of this buttery frosting makes it wonderfully compatible with plain chocolate cakes, in particular the Home-Style Chocolate Cake (page 22), Birthday Buttermilk Chocolate Cake (page 38), Hurry-Up Chocolate Cake (page 66), and Rich Mocha Cake (page 84).

¼ cup strong hot coffee
2 teaspoons instant coffee powder
1 tablespoon coffee liqueur (such as Kahlúa or Tia Maria)
6 tablespoons (¾ stick) unsalted butter, softened
1 teaspoon vanilla extract
4½ cups (1 pound plus *½ cup)* unsifted *confectioners' sugar*

Blend together the coffee, coffee powder, and coffee liqueur in a large mixing bowl. Add the butter and vanilla extract, and let stand for 5 minutes. The instant coffee should be dissolved at this point. Beat in 1½ cups of the confectioners' sugar. Beat in the remaining confectioners' sugar with a hand-held electric mixer, 1 cup at a time, blending thoroughly after each addition. Beat the frosting on high speed for 2 to 3 minutes, or until light.

Use the frosting immediately on thoroughly cooled layer and sheet cakes.

8

Festive Cake Decorating

For a celebration, a cake trimmed with all kinds of embellishments and flourishes makes a merry presentation. Both layer and sheet cakes can be trimmed with graceful swags, swirls, rosettes, and bows using a contrasting (or same shade) frosting pressed through a pastry bag fitted with a decorative tip. Or, you can press simple, edible garnishes onto the surface of the iced or frosted cake.

To decorate a cake using a frosting and a pastry bag, select one of the more substantial frostings in this book, such as the Full of Chocolate Frosting (page 95), Vanilla Butter Frosting (page 101), Brown Sugar Butter Frosting (page 102), Creamy Coffee Frosting (page 106), or Butter and Cream Chocolate Frosting (page 99). You may have to adjust its density by adding more liquid (1 teaspoon at a time) or confectioners' sugar (1 tablespoon at a time) to arrive at the proper piping consistency. For rosettes, ruffles, and swirls, the frosting should be pliant enough to push out of the bag but firm enough to hold its shape. For writing, it must be fluid enough to flow properly and maintain its contour at the same time.

When selecting decorating bags, choose a lightweight variety, preferably the 10- or 12-inch size for easy handling. Assorted tips can be purchased in sets, and a chart is usually included in the collection that identifies the particular shape each tip creates. (As a quick survey, small round tips [Nos. 2, 3, and 4] are useful for writing; there are small, medium, and large tips for drop flowers; tips for ruffled borders or shell borders; tips for petals and leaves; tops for stars, and so on.) You'll also need a coupler, which fits onto both the tip and the decorating bag and serves to hold the tip in place. The coupler also allows you the opportunity to change tips as you wish, without disturbing the contents of the bag.

To outfit the bag with a tip, first unscrew the ring from the coupler and place the coupler in the bottom of the bag, pressing it out through the narrow opening (depending upon the size of the bag, about ¾ inch, more or less, of the coupler will show through). Position the selected tip on the base of the coupler and secure by slipping the plastic ring (or band) over it and turning it until it is tight and in place.

To fill the bag with frosting and create decorations, first twist the bottom of the pastry bag a few times, and press this part into the cavity toward the tip. Make a temporary collar by folding back 1 inch of the top of the pastry bag. Holding the inside cuff of the collar with one hand, fill the bag no more than one-half to two-thirds full with frosting. Flip up the cuff, hold the top with one hand, release the twisted base, and carefully begin to press the frosting down to the base of the tip, using your fingertips by applying light pressure to the outside of the pastry bag. Now gently twist the top to close. With one hand positioned at the top of the twist and the other at the base near the top of the tip, hold the bag at about a 45-degree angle, barely touching the surface of the cake, and apply pressure to press out the frosting. Decorations should be applied to a cake with a smoothly frosted surface. Instead of spreading the frosting in lavish peaks and swirls, sweep it onto the cake in a level, uniform coating, to make an even covering.

For colorful piped decorations, the Vanilla Butter Frosting (page 101) can be tinted with paste icing colors. Concentrated paste colors are available in small 1-ounce jars, in a range of hues. To tint the frosting, place the basic vanilla frosting in a bowl (or bowls); using a toothpick, add the tiniest dot of color to the frosting and blend well. Remember that just a fleck or two of the paste will color the frosting, and the color becomes more vivid on standing. Since an exact color is difficult to re-create, always make a little more of each batch of colored frosting than you think you'll need.

To lend an extravagant look to a layer cake or sheet cake, without ever manipulating a pastry bag, consider these luxurious trimmings for a frosted cake:

Glazed, preserved fruit, whole, in slivers, plain or chocolate-dipped
Rim the perimeter of the cake with slivers or sections of the fruit.

Chocolate pastilles
Round disks of milk or bittersweet chocolate look attractive pressed onto the sides of a layer cake, or angled around the top edge.

Mocha beans
Coffee-flavored chocolate pellets that are made to resemble coffee beans are a delicious accent to chocolate cakes. Lace them in a pattern on the top of the cake, or in a jewel-like ring at the base.

Chocolate-dipped fresh fruit or nuts
Place orange sections or whole strawberries, pecan or walnut halves, dipped in a good chocolate glaze and set aside to firm up, around the border of a cake.

Chocolate twigs

These are lengths of chocolate molded to resemble real twigs, available boxed in the candy section of some markets and food emporiums. Pile them in the middle of a cake, like pickup sticks, for a dramatic effect.

Chocolate bark

Break up pieces of bark candy (plain, chocolate-nut, or chocolate-coconut) and press them around the sides of a frosted layer cake.

Nut brittle

Crush nut brittle (peanut, pecan, macadamia) and press it around the sides of a frosted layer cake.

Marzipan

Marzipan candies, tinted and molded into all kinds of shapes (from fruits to vegetables, figures, and more), are available at specialty food emporiums. Place these strategically on the top or at the base of a layer cake.

Sprinkles, miniature candies, and such

Seasonal sprinkles (color-coded for Halloween, Easter, Christmas) and miniature candies (chocolate drops, baby peanut butter nuggets, milk chocolate kisses, toffee chips and chunks, two-bite candy bars, licorice bits, and spice drops) delight children and can be used recklessly on sheet cakes. Avoid any attempt at restraint. This decorated cake is ideal to take to school for a birthday celebration.

Index